RAND

Private Giving to Public Schools and Districts in Los Angeles County

A Pilot Study

Ron Zimmer, Cathy Krop, Tessa Kaganoff, Karen E. Ross, Dominic J. Brewer

Prepared for the
John Randolph and Dora Haynes Foundation

RAND Education

The research described in this report was prepared for the John Randolph and Dora Haynes Foundation.

Library of Congress Cataloging-in-Publication Data

Private giving to public schools and districts in Los Angeles County : a pilot study / Ron Zimmer ... [et al.].
       p. cm.
       "MR-1429."
       Includes bibliographical references.
       ISBN 0-8330-3066-3
       1. Public schools—California—Los Angeles County—Finance. 2. School districts—California—Los Angeles County—Finance. 3. Educational fund raising—California—Los Angeles County. I. Zimmer, Ron W.

LB2826.C2 P75 2001
379.1'1—dc21

2001048343

Published 2001 by RAND
1700 Main Street, P.O. Box 2138, Santa Monica, CA 90407-2138
1200 South Hayes Street, Arlington, VA 22202-5050
201 North Craig Street, Suite 102, Pittsburgh, PA 15213
RAND URL: http://www.rand.org/
To order RAND documents or to obtain additional information, contact Distribution Services: Telephone: (310) 451-7002; Fax: (310) 451-6915; Email: order@rand.org

Preface

This report presents the results of RAND's pilot study on how Los Angeles–area public schools and school districts secure support from private sources. The study was commissioned by the John Randolph and Dora Haynes Foundation, which supports research within the greater Los Angeles region on social science issues with policy implications.

The authors sought to answer questions in three major areas regarding support for schools and school districts: (1) Who are the private givers to public education? (2) How do schools and school districts attract private support—through school-based organizations or through school and district personnel—and what mechanisms do schools and districts use to attract private resources? (3) What types of support are provided and how are the contributions used? The results presented in this report are based on interviews conducted in fall and winter 2000 with superintendents and school district staff, school principals, and local education foundation (LEF) representatives.

This report is directed to multiple audiences. First, the findings in this report will help district, school, and LEF personnel plan for and assess the role of private support in their schools and districts. Second, businesses and foundations can use this report to make decisions on how best to support public education. And third, policymakers can develop better strategies for supporting the schools' efforts to secure support.

Contents

Tables

Summary

The nation's public schools have been under attack over much of the past three decades. A commonly heard criticism is that school performance, as measured by students' standardized test scores, has stagnated or declined over the years. At the same time, schools have failed to close the gap in achievement between the lowest-performing and highest-performing students. This situation exists despite increased resources for public schools and attempts to allocate resources more equitably.

Dependence on state support has created a number of concerns for the nation's schools and school districts. School finance reforms have led to increased decisionmaking at the state level regarding education at a time when governance reforms call for more local control. State decisionmaking, in turn, imposes constraints on local decisionmaking. Schools have become dependent on the state economy and must compete with other demands on state resources. In addition, state education funding over time has shifted toward a greater reliance on categorical (that is, restricted) funds and a lesser reliance on general-purpose (that is, flexible) funds.

Taken together, reforms in school finance and education governance have made securing private support for public education an important activity of many public schools and districts. While public schools and districts have always attracted private support, anecdotal reports and a limited body of documented research suggest they are now pursuing private support with increased sophistication and aggressiveness.

Current reports and research provide a limited accounting of private support of public education and no systematic framework for thinking about such support. This pilot study is designed to provide schools and school districts with information on the types of public-private partnerships that have been developed and the mechanisms used to attract private resources.

In addition, we are interested in documenting the types of monetary and in-kind resources[1] that are most likely to be available to schools and districts that have differing economic resources within their communities.

---

[1]*In-kind support* includes volunteer time and donated materials, equipment, and supplies. *Monetary support* is financial support for a specified or unspecified purpose.

This report focuses on questions relating to three broad areas:

1. Who are the private givers to public education?

2. How do schools and districts attract private support—through school-based organizations or through school and district personnel—and what mechanisms do schools and districts use to attract private resources?

3. What types of support are provided, and how are the contributions used?

To address these "who, how, and what" questions, we collected data from interviews with school and district staff and from questionnaires distributed to ten elementary schools in six districts in Los Angeles County.[2] The county provides a field of richly diverse districts and schools. Within the county, we picked a sample of schools and districts operating under different governance structures in communities that differ socioeconomically, and we selected districts of various sizes.

The information in this report should be useful to districts and schools in helping them plan for and assess the role of private support of public education. In addition, businesses and foundations can use our research to make decisions regarding how best to support public education. In particular, private corporations and foundations may be interested in learning how other similar organizations are supporting public education and which types of resources provide the most leverage for gaining private support.

This report represents our effort to better understand private support, both in-kind and monetary, in public education. We identify successful strategies for maximizing support and for overcoming obstacles in obtaining funding for public schools.

The Who, How, and What of Private Giving

To systematically examine private giving at the sample schools and districts, we developed a matrix that presents a useful framework for examining the various dimensions of private giving. The matrix includes private givers, school or district-based entities channeling private resources, mechanisms to attract private resources, types of private giving, and the use of private monetary giving. Specifically, both monetary and in-kind resources flow from private givers through various entities, and those entities attract donations through a variety of

---

[2]In the interest of maintaining anonymity, the specific names of the schools and school districts that participated in the study are not listed in this report.

mechanisms. Private giving, in turn, may take a variety of forms and be used for diverse purposes.

Within each dimension of private giving, we developed a comprehensive list of different examples of givers, mechanisms to attract private support, types of gifts, and uses of gifts. For instance, for private givers, the list of examples includes parents and local businesses, to name just a couple. These examples came from an extensive literature review, site visits, and interviews with school and district staff. We then examined the data for each district and school in our sample to determine whether we saw evidence of each example at a particular site.

Who Are the Private Givers?

Whereas parental involvement was the most common form of "giving" at the school level, other contributors played a significant role in providing support to the schools. A majority of schools rely on parents, local businesses, corporations, and community-based organizations for support. Although not as prevalent across schools, for 25 to 50 percent of the sample schools, students, philanthropic foundations, community members, professional associations, and city governments are givers (and often donate gifts of significant size). In contrast, colleges and universities did not play an active role in our sample schools.

Our sample districts attracted support from many of the same private givers as our sample schools, although the size of those contributions differed. Overall, school districts tended to attract resources from larger and more-organized groups, such as corporations, local businesses, and colleges and universities, as opposed to obtaining resources from individuals and smaller groups and associations, which was typical at the school level.

School or District-Based Entities Channeling Private Resources

At all of the sample schools, the principal was involved to some degree in attracting private resources to his or her school. In general, it was the principal who took the lead in developing relationships and maintaining ongoing communication with the community at large and other private sponsors. In addition, the principal was often a school's sole connection with its business and community sponsors. The majority of schools also enlisted Parent-Teacher Associations (PTAs) and local education foundations (LEFs) to attract private support. Whereas seven of the schools cited the existence of a district LEF, only one school regarded the LEF as a significant player in attracting private support.

Each of the districts had district staff at some level responsible for private giving. The district interviewees generally stated that the district staff played a variety of roles in helping schools attract private support (for example, in organizing special events, establishing school-business partnerships, or providing grant-writing assistance). However, the schools were generally not well informed about district activities.

Mechanisms to Attract Private Resources

The mechanisms that schools relied on most heavily to attract private in-kind and monetary resources were personal contacts and relationship building, product sales, and special events. Almost every school principal emphasized the importance of personal contacts and relationship building in attracting private resources. A smaller portion of the schools that we visited relied on mail solicitations, grant applications, and school-business partnerships, but those mechanisms were key components of their strategy to attract private resources.

Superintendents and district-level staff also relied heavily on personal contacts and relationship building to attract private resources. The next most prevalent strategies at the district level were grant applications and development of school-business partnerships.

Although the districts actively raise support, the principals whom we interviewed consistently reported that the share of private resources that the schools themselves raise is greater than the share they receive from the districts.

Types of Private Giving

We divided private giving into three types: volunteer time, material donations, and monetary contributions.

At the school level, no one volunteer activity appeared to dominate across the schools; different schools received different kinds of volunteer support. Volunteers gave their time to such activities as tutoring programs, after-school enrichment programs, mentoring programs, and classroom support.

The majority of schools received donations of instructional materials, computers and software, equipment and supplies, and gift certificates and awards (such as free tickets to a ball game for an outstanding report card). In addition, the vast majority of schools received some level of monetary donation from a variety of private givers. Our interview respondents suggested that corporate and business donors generally start out by providing in-kind support and, as the relationships developed, some givers would eventually provide monetary support as well.

Monetary donations were almost always targeted for a specific purpose or program. Generally, schools first developed priorities, plans, or goals and then approached private givers with specific proposals. The use of private monetary support, therefore, was not totally flexible in that the monies were given to support a specific program or goal. Relatively small amounts of money received through a variety of "percent of sales " programs (such as a major retailer donating a portion of its sales of a particular product) were truly flexible in terms of how they could be used.

School principals had a difficult time quantifying the levels of both in-kind and monetary support, and in particular in-kind support. With that said, school principals uniformly agreed that in-kind support significantly outweighs monetary support in quantity. In addition, principals generally put greater value on in-kind support (especially volunteer support) than monetary support.

The districts in the sample generally attracted less volunteer time and fewer material donations than the schools, and therefore concentrated more heavily on monetary donations. About one-half of the districts did, however, receive volunteer support for family services that were provided at the school level. Districts, more so than the schools, generally focused on pursuing monetary donations from larger givers in order to support larger-scale, district-wide programs. Neither districts nor schools obtained paid endorsements or advertising revenue, and the majority of schools and districts explicitly stated that they restrict paid endorsements.

Use of Private Monetary Giving

Private monetary giving supports a wide range of activities that tend to fall into three main categories: current operations, technology, and capital improvements.

Schools used private monetary support most often on curricular enrichment activities, such as field trips and after-school programs. The majority of schools also used private dollars for school supplies and equipment and non-teacher staff salaries. Private monetary support generally was intended to be used in the short term, which affected how schools decided to use this support.

Districts most often used privately donated money to support curricular enrichment programs, purchase instructional material, and support professional development. A majority of districts also used private monetary support to purchase computers and other technology. When deciding how to allocate funds or resources to schools, district staff generally stated that they distribute money according to where the greatest need exists.

Differences in Support for Schools and Districts by Socioeconomic Status

We observed some differences in the nature of private giving in schools and school districts depending on their socioeconomic status.[3] Schools located in the wealthiest communities (that is, those with the highest socioeconomic status) had very strong parental support in absolute terms, relative to other schools in the sample. While there was a greater level of parental support at schools in wealthier communities, some schools in the poorer communities were also successful in raising private support, although they needed to approach a relatively wide array of private donors. The list of private givers was relatively longer for some of the lower socioeconomic schools also because those schools had options to attract private giving that were not available in the more-affluent communities. For example, many foundations and large corporations are more willing to provide resources to schools in poorer communities because of the perceived greater needs of those schools.

As mechanisms for attracting private support, developing personal contacts and relationship building appear to be particularly important to schools in the middle and lower socioeconomic communities. Those schools could not as readily rely on parental monetary and in-kind support as schools in the wealthier communities. Instead, in order to attract private support, they were dependent on a dynamic school principal who was interested in making contacts in the community to attract and maintain private support.

The wealthier schools had a strong focus on direct monetary donations, particularly from parents. At the same time, even the wealthiest schools in our sample reported that private monetary contributions accounted for less than 5 percent of their total budgets. The wealthier schools also received sizable in-kind contributions from parents volunteering their time at the schools. Schools located in communities in the middle or lower socioeconomic strata appeared to have at least as much in-kind private support as the wealthier communities, but the support came from different types of private givers. Although is difficult to get a

---

[3]We measured socioeconomic status by the percentage of students who participate in the federally funded Free and Reduced Price Lunch Program. Schools with the highest socioeconomic status in our study had the fewest participants in the program, whereas schools with the lowest socioeconomic status had the most participants.

sense of the relative size of the in-kind contributions because volunteer time is difficult to measure, the variety of private givers who contributed their time to the schools was greater in the middle- level and lower-level socioeconomic communities.

The relatively large size of monetary donations received by the two sample schools in the wealthiest communities was evident in the number and type of items the schools bought with the donations. In addition, although LEFs were found across districts of various wealth in our sample, the two highest-income districts had especially active LEFs.

Similar to what was observed at the school level, the higher-income districts relied most heavily on monetary donations, whereas the lower- and middle-income districts received a relatively large number of in-kind donations. The wealthier the district, the more programs, services, and materials the district could purchase with private monetary contributions.

Lessons Learned: Recommended Strategies for Securing Private Support

From our analyses, we are able to offer both broad strategies for securing private support for public schools and more-focused strategies for meeting specific challenges in raising private support for public education.

Broad-Based Strategies for Raising Private Support

The recommendations that follow offer some general strategies for raising support for public education.

Maintain Continual Communication. One comment that we heard from all districts and schools related to the importance of continual communication with the community at large.

Make It a Reciprocal Relationship. Both school and district officials noted the importance of creating a reciprocal relationship with business partners so that both parties feel they are benefiting from the relationship.

Finds Ways for Donors to "Get Their Feet Wet." Several school principals noted that one effective strategy is to find ways for community members to make modest contributions to support a school, and thereby get them introduced to the school and its needs. Once volunteers saw what was happening at the schools and got to know the students, they frequently came back with more support.

Make It Appealing for Individuals and Organizations to Become Involved.
Districts and schools reported that they needed to be flexible and creative in their
approach to making involvement appealing to prospective donors. In addition,
several respondents stated that successful schools make everyone feel welcome.

Provide Training to Volunteers. Another effective strategy used by some schools
was to provide orientation or training to community members who were interested in volunteering at the schools.

Know Your Resource Base. Representatives from the schools and districts discussed how the various characteristics of their communities affected how they
approached raising private support. They suggested that identifying their resource base required a good understanding of their communities and what they
had to offer in terms of support.

Private Support Garners More Private Support. Staff members from several
districts and schools noted that when a school or district can establish some credibility with potential givers, other givers (including foundations, corporations,
and the like) are more willing to give.

The Challenges of Raising Private Support and Suggested Strategies

Schools and districts employed a variety of tactics to overcome some of the
difficult challenges they faced in raising and maintaining private support.

Time Demands. At every school in the sample, most of the responsibility for raising private support rested with the principal. One school addressed this problem
by seeking a grant to pay the salary of a community liaison to assist the principal.

Turnover and Mobility. One of the challenges districts and schools consistently
faced was turnover of key district or school staff and turnover of key contacts at
local businesses. One way to address this issue is to get more than one person involved at both the school or district level and business level. One district even
formalized its relationship with supporting businesses through written contracts.

Short-term Support Mentality. In almost every case, district and school staff
members noted that donors regarded donations and in-kind gifts as short-term
commitments and not part of an ongoing program of giving. Developing an informal verbal "contract" with donors that specifies the level and type of giving
may create a longer-term commitment.

Not Knowing How to Attract Private Support. Several school principals reported that they lacked knowledge on how to raise private support, and weren't sure how to go about gaining that knowledge. Several districts addressed this problem by making district staff available to schools within the district.

Lack of Communication Between Districts and Schools. Schools seemed to have limited knowledge of services or programs pertaining to raising private support that are available from their districts. The communication problem was successfully addressed by one district that hosts monthly meetings with the school principals, PTA presidents, and LEF director in the district.

"Donor Fatigue. " District staff and principals complained that competition among schools and fund-raising organizations resulted in local businesses being approached by multiple sources for help at the same time. Monthly meetings, mentioned in the previous strategy, not only facilitated internal communication, but also helped ensure that multiple parties were not approaching the same donor simultaneously.

Fear of Commercialization. Many district and school staff members expressed concern over the possibility of inappropriate business activities within the schools. For this reason, most districts and schools avoided exclusivity contracts with business enterprises.

Future Research

The analysis in this report offers a large step forward in our knowledge of the relationships between communities and public schools. Nevertheless, we can continue to build on this knowledge with future research. First and foremost, future research should include a larger sample of schools, which could provide a more-representative cross-section and allow for statistical analysis of differences across schools and communities. A larger sample would also allow for an examination across a number of geographic areas beyond Los Angeles County. Patterns of giving and uses of gifts may vary across different geographic areas, which may bring greater insights into the range of relationships existing between communities and public schools.

Second, future research should include development of a survey that specifically probes districts and principals about monetary contributions, volunteer time, and in-kind gifts given to the districts and schools. Although school officials may not know exactly how much is given to a district or to schools, a survey that includes at least a range of dollar values for monetary contributions would serve to improve the existing data. In addition, the survey should probe for the various types of volunteer activities, and probe for a range of the number of hours spent by volunteers in those activities, and the quality of those hours. In addition, the survey should specifically ask school officials to provide an estimated value of in-kind gifts. Among other benefits, this information would provide a clearer picture of the degree to which districts and schools are circumventing, or not circumventing, equalized funding systems through private contributions.

Third, future research should include interviews with donors. By conducting such interviews, greater insight into why people and organizations give, and why businesses and organizations choose certain schools to support, may be gained. These interviews may also serve to verify the value of making contributions to schools.

Finally, future research should place a greater emphasis on business partnerships. More-extensive research into business partnerships would provide additional insight into how these relationships get started in the first place and how they mature over time.

Acknowledgments

We wish to express our thanks to the superintendents, district staff, school principals, and local education foundation representatives who shared their time and insights with us. We also wish to thank Eiko Moriyama, Gloria Mamokhin, Howie Schaffer, and Eric Brunner for their thoughts on private giving to public schools.

Cassie Guarino and Larry Picus provided thoughtful and constructive reviews that greatly enhanced the analysis and report, Kristen Leuschner improved the report through her contributions to the writing, Claudia Szabo assisted with formatting an earlier version of this report, and Nancy DelFavero edited the final report.

Despite the assistance of so many, we, the authors, take full responsibility for any errors that may remain.

Acronyms

BSR	Business for Social Responsibility
CCD	Common core data
CCEF	California Consortium of Education Foundations
CDE	California Department of Education
LAEP	Los Angeles Educational Partnership
LAUSD	Los Angeles Unified School District
LEF	Local education foundation
NCES	National Center for Education Statistics
NPR	National percentile ranking
PEN	Public Education Network
PTA	Parent-Teacher Association
PTO	Parent-Teacher Organization
RFP	Request for proposal
STAR	Standardized Testing and Reporting

1. Introduction

The nation's public schools have been under attack for much of the past three decades. A common criticism is that their performance, as measured by students' standardized test scores, has been stagnant or declining. At the same time, schools have failed to close the gap in achievement between the lowest- and highest-performing students. These developments have occurred despite the increase in resources given to public schools and attempts to allocate those resources more equitably.

Real per-pupil expenditures nationwide increased from \$1,973 to \$6,146 between 1960 and 1996 (National Center for Education Statistics, 1999). In addition, since the 1970s, more than 34 states have faced legal challenges to their school funding systems in an effort to achieve greater equity in the distribution of education dollars (Dayton, 2000). Policymakers at the state level across the country have responded to these legal challenges by moving away from the traditional dependence on local property taxes for school funding toward greater dependence on state support.[1]

Reforms in governance and finance have made raising private support an important activity of many public schools and school districts. A major wave of education reform over the past decade calls for improving the quality of education nationwide through changes in the governance structures of educational systems. This movement, which includes site-based management and charter school reforms, decentralizes public education decisionmaking to more-local levels of control. The governance reforms are based on the concept that education can be improved by allowing those closest to students to make policy decisions based on the characteristics of the local community.[2]

---

[1]Most of the efforts at equalizing funding have focused on equalizing funding across districts in a *state*. Some more-recent efforts have focused on equalizing funding across schools in a *district*. For example, the Rodriguez consent degree operating in the Los Angeles Unified School District seeks to equalize educational opportunities across schools within the district.

[2]During the twentieth century, structural changes occurred in education provision that weakened the relationship between public schools and their local communities. During the Great Depression of the 1930s, budgets became tight and school districts and states began to look for ways to cut costs. One mechanism for cutting costs was the consolidation of public school districts (Pugh, 1994). For example, between 1940 and 1950, the number of school districts in the country dropped from 117,108 to 83,718. This trend continued, although at a slower pace, through the second half of the twentieth century, with the number of school districts nationwide dropping to just under 15,000 by 1997.

School finance reforms, on the other hand, have led to more education decision-making at the state level at a time when governance reforms call for more local control. State decisionmaking imposes a number of constraints on local decisionmaking. Schools become dependent on their state's economy and must compete with other demands on state resources. In addition, state aid over time has shifted toward a greater reliance on categorical (that is, restricted) funds and a lesser reliance on general purpose (that is, flexible) funds.[3]

Although the movement toward equalized funding across schools through funding from the state has lead to greater resources for some schools, state funding for other schools has been constrained due to the local taxpayers' desire to keep funding for public education at a certain level. Some researchers have suggested that these fiscal constraints have forced schools to look for alternative sources of funding. One such alternative is found in private contributions (Brunner and Sonstelie, 1999; Addonizio, 1999).

While public schools and districts have always attracted private support, anecdotal reports and a limited body of documented research suggest they are pursuing private support with increased sophistication and aggressiveness. Public schools and school districts increasingly are looking to private support to maintain the quality of schooling during periods when public revenues are tight due to the current political climate.[4]

Private funding also provides a way to increase flexibility in how educational funds are spent at the local level, and it allows families to match their demand for education (that is, their willingness to pay for education through taxes and other payments) to the preferred level of education for their children.[5] However, if certain schools and districts are more successful than others in raising private support, any existing inequities may be exacerbated.

Private support of public education is an important policy issue that goes beyond matters of equity. It is likely that all school communities have both monetary and

---

[3]Evidence of this shift occurring in California is found in the Legislative Analyst's Office (2000) document.

[4]According to a recent study, diminishing tax receipts were the major reason that a majority of nonprofit local education foundations were formed in California, Massachusetts, Oregon, Illinois, and Washington (Merz and Frankel, 1995).

[5]In response to the 1971 decision in *Serrano v. Priest*, California legislators assigned a spending cap across school districts to help equalize funding. Due to this spending limit, Fischel (1992) suggests that families are not able to achieve their individual preferences given the level of educational expenditures (that is, tax dollars). Traditionally, a family could satisfy its preferences for larger educational expenditures by locating in a district with a higher spending level for education. However, with spending caps, a family that has a strong preference for larger expenditures cannot achieve the educational level desired.

in-kind[6] resources that can be leveraged in support of education; we simply may not have identified them yet, or figured out how to measure them. Presumably, practices exist to enlist private support that can and will transcend income levels and community differences. At the same time, it is likely that certain types of private support are more or less accessible in different types of communities. Identifying available monetary and in-kind resources, and the mechanisms that are available to gain private support, can be valuable information for education practitioners.

To explore some of the issues surrounding support of education, we conducted a study of private support of public education in Los Angeles County. This research is considered a pilot study because it is small in scale and has, in part, contributed to developing the tools, initial findings, and hypotheses needed to guide further analyses. Specifically, the study was designed to provide schools and districts with information on the types of public-private partnerships that have been developed in various communities and the mechanisms used to attract private resources. In addition, we are interested in documenting the types of monetary and in-kind resources that are most likely to be available to schools and districts with differing economic resources.

We set out to answer a number of questions with this study. For instance, who are the private givers to public education? Are they exclusively parents of schoolchildren and large corporations, or are other individuals and organizations significant supporters? In this regard, we documented the range of organizations and individuals from which private support originates.

In addition, what role do school and district organizations and individuals—such as Parent-Teacher Associations (PTAs), local education foundations (LEFs), and school and district staff—play in attracting private support? What is the range of mechanisms that organizations and individuals use to attract private support?

Do schools rely primarily on product sales, or are special events and business partnerships their primary means of attracting private support?

Finally, what is the ultimate use of both monetary and in-kind gifts? Do private contributions support payment of salaries, purchasing of school supplies, enhancement of school facilities, or support of special programs?

Taken together, all of the questions just posed can be summarized within three broad areas:

---

[6]*In-kind support* includes volunteer time and donated materials, equipment, and supplies. *Monetary support* is financial support for a specified or unspecified purpose.

1. Who are the private givers to public education?

2. How do schools and districts attract private support—through school-based organizations or through school and district personnel—and what mechanisms do schools and districts use to attract private resources?

3. What types of support are provided, and how are the contributions used?

Current media reports and research studies provide a limited accounting of private support of public education and no systematic framework for thinking about such support.[7] Media reports by and large provide anecdotal evidence of private support and document funding success stories. A large portion of the recent research literature focuses on private monetary support of public education by LEFs and any inequities that this type of support may create. Whereas LEFs are clearly an important component of private support, they represent only one type of private support available to public education.

In addition, national and state databases generally do not list the types and amounts of private giving in detail. When the data sets do account for private monetary donations, that information is typically lumped together under a category called "other revenues." Furthermore, whereas Internal Revenue Service data do include some financial information on nonprofit organizations, such as LEFs or PTAs operating in conjunction with public schools, these data include only those organizations that secure relatively high levels of private monetary support.

To address our "who, how, and what" questions, we collected data through interviews with school principals and district superintendents and staff and questionnaires distributed to staff at ten elementary schools in six districts in Los Angeles County,[8] and from an examination of the literature. We focused initially on elementary schools because previous research suggests that organizations associated with those schools tend to raise the most revenue per pupil, and because volunteer involvement is greatest at the elementary level (Merz and Frankel, 1995). Los Angeles County provides a field of richly diverse districts and schools. In addition, it includes urban areas that experience many of the problems typically faced by failing school districts. Within the county, we picked a sample of schools and districts operating under different governance structures in communities that differ socioeconomically, and we selected districts of different sizes.

---

[7]See Chapter 2 for a review of this literature.

[8]In the interest of maintaining anonymity, the specific names of the schools and school districts that participated in our study are not listed in this report.

Our results suggest that a variety of school and district-based organizations are using various mechanisms to channel monetary and in-kind support to public education from a wide range of private givers. Differences exist in private giving at both the school and district level in general, with schools focusing more closely on parental support and districts focusing more closely on support from organized groups, including corporations.

Among schools, those that are located in the wealthier communities have a greater level of parental monetary and in-kind support. However, this does not necessarily translate into greater overall support. Oftentimes, because of their perceived need, districts and schools in lower-income areas have greater access to support from corporations and community-based and philanthropic organizations. Therefore, we did not find strong evidence that private contributions necessarily lead to greater inequities in the support of public schools.

In all districts and schools, gaining private support requires developing, maintaining, and engaging in reciprocal relationships with private sponsors, activities that take time and personal commitment. Currently, most of the responsibility for developing private support at the school level is assumed by the school principal, particularly in lower-income communities. Additionally, districts and schools that pursue private support may encounter a number of obstacles, including how to find the time to conduct efforts to gain support, and dealing with turnover of district and school staff or turnover at partnering organizations. To overcome these obstacles, districts and schools can institute a variety of measures, which we discuss in Chapter 5.

In Chapter 2, we highlight what we currently know, based on the existing literature, about who the givers are, what they give and why, and how districts and schools can gain support. Chapter 3 discusses our methodology for addressing the questions raised in Chapter 2. Chapter 4 provides the results of our analysis, and Chapter 5 offers our conclusions and the implications from our analysis.

2. What We Currently Know About Private Support of Public Education

Although the research literature has grown in recent years, most of what we know about private support of public education comes from anecdotal reports generated by the news media. Over the past decade, newspapers across the country have documented volunteer efforts and covered stories on districts forming independent local education foundations. Most of this coverage consists of reports on the various activities that take place at certain schools or districts and their successful efforts.[1] The recent research literature, on the other hand, has focused primarily on monetary support raised by local education foundations and other school-based organizations.

In this chapter, we highlight what the literature has told us about private support for public education. We first discuss some of the historical and recent trends that are creating the current impetus for private support. We then discuss theories on *why* people and organizations give. Next, we describe the literature related to the three general questions surrounding our research: (1) *Who* are the givers; (2) *how* do they attract private support; and (3) *what* do they give and for what purpose? These three questions serve to describe the flow of gift-giving from donors to the end users of gifts, and serve as the basis for the analyses discussed in later chapters of this report.

Historical Trends

Private support of public schools is not a new development. Schools and school districts have long relied on private monetary and in-kind support, in addition to federal, state, and local tax revenues. PTAs, classroom volunteers, booster clubs, and school-business relationships, for example, have traditionally been associated with public schools. Yet, recent media accounts and a handful of research studies suggest that the schools and school districts are pursuing private support with increased sophistication and aggressiveness.

The impetus for greater levels of private support comes largely from the convergence of changes in the states' school finance systems and changes in school

---

[1]See, for example, Anderson (1997), Helman (2000), Benning (1999), and Mount (1993).

governance models. Since the 1970s, more than 34 states have faced legal challenges to their school funding systems (Dayton, 2000). These challenges have been based on language contained in state constitutions regarding equitable educational opportunities for all students. In response to these challenges, to achieve greater equity in the use of dollars for education, school funding in many states has moved away from its traditional dependence on local property taxes toward greater dependence on state support.

As shown in Table 2.1, as of 1997, states represent the largest portion of public education funding, at 48 percent, with local school districts providing 45.5 percent of funding. Many states have experienced taxpayer revolts of varying magnitude in the form of tax rollback initiatives, tax-limitation measures, and spending caps (Mullins and Joyce, 1996). And, although support for education has shifted to the states, difficult economic times of varying intensity in some states have meant lower state revenues and tight budgets for education.

California is a case in point. In a landmark 1971 case, *Serrano v. Priest*, the California State Supreme Court ruled that the substantial per-pupil revenue differences that resulted from reliance on property taxes were unconstitutional. Later, in 1978, the residents of California passed Proposition 13, which limited the ability of local school districts to tax residents to raise revenues for support of schools. The combined effects of court-imposed school finance equalization and the local property tax limitation measure have led to a centralized state system of school finance in California. Critics have argued that, together, these decisions

Table 2.1

Dollar and Percentage Distribution of Funding for Public Schools (1997 dollars)

	Federal		State		Local	
Year	Amount ($M)	Percentage	Amount ($M)	Percentage	Amount ($M)	Percentage
1920	2	0.3	160	16.5	808	83.2
1930	7	0.4	354	16.9	1,728	82.7
1940	40	1.8	684	30.3	1,536	68.0
1950	156	2.9	2,166	39.8	3,116	57.3
1960	652	4.4	5,768	39.1	8,327	56.5
1970	3,220	8.0	16,063	39.9	20,985	52.1
1980	6,504	9.8	45,349	46.8	42,029	43.4
1990	12,701	6.1	98,239	47.1	97,608	46.8
1997	20,081	6.5	146,434	48.0	138,537	45.5

Source: National Center for Education Statistics (1999), Table 154.

have caused California to go from being one of the highest per-pupil spending states to one of the lowest.[2] When a recession hit California in the early 1990s, the real effects of state-controlled school finance began to be felt, with per-pupil spending for schools dropping from the fifth highest in the nation in the mid-1980s to the forty-second highest in 1995.

Why People Give

Private support to public schools has been a steadfast tradition throughout the history of public schooling in the United States. As with other forms of charitable giving, it raises the question, why are people willing to donate both their time and their money? From a benefit-cost perspective, it is sometimes difficult to understand the incentives of givers of private support, especially when the support is monetary.[3] Because this question goes beyond just giving to public schools, it has led economists and other researchers to explore the reasons why people and organizations engage in altruistic behavior.

Two prevailing economic theories on why individuals give consist of a *public-good model* and a *private-consumption model* (Duncan, 1999).

The public-good model suggests that individuals give in order to increase the provision of a public good.[4] However, this explanation begs a second question: Why would a person give to a cause if the individual contribution, which is generally relatively small, might not significantly affect the total provision of the public good?[5] Some researchers have answered this question by suggesting that penalties exist for being a "free-rider." For example, if a person is a member of an

---

[2]A number of research papers have linked equity reform to the decline in spending per pupil. Fischel (1989, 1992, and 1993) argues that the elimination of local control over spending may lead to a reduction in popular support for education and translate into reduced total spending for education. Theobald and Picus (1991) argue that centralizing funding will force education to compete with other state expenditures for funds and, as a result, the growth rate of spending per pupil will decrease over time. Silva and Sonstelie (1993) offer a hypothesis linking reform to the decline in spending per pupil. Fernandez and Rogerson (1995) provide a related theory. Despite this growing body of research that suggests centralized funding will slow the growth of educational expenditures and support for education, there is dissension from this view. Hickrod et al. (1992) and Manwaring and Sheffrin (1995) argue that the growth rate for educational expenditures may increase as a result of the movement toward centralized funding. Manwaring and Sheffrin argue that spending on education could increase because educational reform has given the issue greater prominence.

[3]Whereas tax deductions are an important consideration for potential donors, they cannot fully explain the reasons behind charitable contributions. The benefits of a tax deduction, by definition, are less than the cost of the gift itself.

[4]In this context, a "public good" can be thought of as any public service.

[5]In many cases, the charitable contribution of an individual is treated unilaterally. In other words, an individual's act of giving occurs without consideration of other people's giving behavior. However, some researchers argue that givers *do* use social interaction in their decision process (Brunner and Sonstelie, 1999). Rather than taking the charitable behavior of others as a given, a contributor considers other givers' behavior and a decision is based on that.

organization that is working toward a specific goal, there may be the expectation that each member will donate a specific amount of resources (that is, money or time) to reach that goal. If the person does not fully give his or her fair share there may be "social penalties" in that others would look down upon an individual who does not contribute what he or she can rightfully afford (Brunner and Sonstelie, 1999).[6]

The private-consumption model also suggests that the reasons why individuals give are not purely altruistic ones. In fact, this model argues that giving is a private good that does, in fact, provide benefits to the giver, such as a "warm glow" or added prestige (Becker, 1974; Andreoni, 1989; Glazer and Konrad, 1996; Harbaugh, 1998). Therefore, unlike with the public-good model, a person's contribution is meaningful because it provides value to the giver whether or not the contribution has some kind of external effect (Duncan, 1999). In fact, Harbaugh (1998) noted that contributors might not even care if the money they give is having any social impact; rather, they care only if it provides personal satisfaction and recognition.[7] In general, the private-consumption model suggests that contributions to charitable organizations can be considered similar to any other goods or services on which people spend their money. No matter their reasons, it is quite clear that many people and organizations give to a variety of causes and services, including public education.

Local businesses and major corporations also engage in altruistic behavior for a number of reasons. The Business for Social Responsibility (BSR) Web site (www.bsr.org) outlines several explanations for corporate involvement in giving, including "increased sales, improved employee morale, an enhanced ability to compete for valued employees in the local labor pool, and being seen as a 'neighbor of choice' in the community." BSR also notes that, increasingly, a range of business stakeholders including investors, customers, employees, public-interest groups, and even government officials are putting pressure on businesses to become involved in their communities and to act as "good citizens." Companies are also motivated by the recognition that they are sometimes in a better position to address certain social problems than are government agencies.

---

[6]Brunner and Sonstelie (1999) suggest that fund-raising organizations, such as Parent-Teacher Organizations, use social interaction as a mechanism for inducing people to give. In other words, these organizations hold events in which interested parties (parents, for example) can observe other people's giving behavior and then make decisions based on that observation.

[7]Harbaugh (1998) suggests that if gaining prestige for themselves motivates donors, organizations can increase donations by reporting categories of donations. Glazer and Konrad (1996) argue further that donations can be a signal of wealth and that people may gain social approval by giving beyond the average donation level.

Who Are the Givers?

In this section, we describe the givers of both in-kind and monetary contributions to schools. Parents have always been a key source of giving to public schools. Parental contributions include straight monetary donations or donations of materials and supplies, but may also include contributions of time for such things as fund-raisers or supporting teachers in the classroom.

As shown in Table 2.2, approximately 20 percent of households[8] across the country contributed an average of about $300 to education in 1995. While a higher percentage of households contribute to several other charitable organizations, education receives a relatively high average annual amount per household.

Currently, the perception exists that money is tight and teachers are stretched thin, so parents are increasingly asked to take on added roles and do more than respond to the traditional school fund-raiser. Many schools are asking parents to have a stronger presence at their children's schools and participate in everything

Table 2.2

Households Contributing to Education and Other Charitable Organizations and Their Average Donation, 1995

| | | Average Annual Contribution | |
Type of Charity	Percentage of Total Households Contributing	Per Contributing Household	Per Total Household
Religious	48.0	$868	$417
Health	27.3	$214	$58
Human services	25.1	$271	$68
Youth development	20.9	$137	$29
Education	20.3	$318	$65
Environment	11.5	$106	$12
Public and societal benefit	10.3	$122	$13
Arts, culture, and humanities	9.4	$216	$20
Recreation, adults	7.0	$161	$11
Private and community foundations	6.1	$181	$11
International, foreign	6.1	$283	$17
Other	2.1	$160	$3

Source: National Center for Education Statistics (1999), Table 30.

---

[8]"Households" do not necessarily include parents or parents of school-age children. In addition, "education" may include both public and private education.

from instructional support and school governance to school maintenance.[9]
However, this may put some districts and schools at a disadvantage. Table 2.3
suggests a positive relationship exists between family income and involvement in
school activities.

To illustrate, 67 to 69 percent of families with incomes up to $25,000 report attending a school meeting, whereas approximately 81 to 88 percent of families
with incomes of more than $40,000 report attending a school meeting. Similarly,
whereas less than 30 percent of parents from relatively low-income households
volunteer at their children's school, around 50 percent of parents from relatively
high-income households volunteer. In addition, single parents, parents who are
employed outside the home, parents who live far from their children's school,
and fathers are involved to a lesser degree, on average, in activities that take
place at the school building.[10]

Table 2.3

**Elementary and Secondary School Children Whose Parents Are Involved in
School Activities**

Annual Family Income	Percentage of Children Whose Parents Report That They . . .			
	Attended a General School Meeting	Attended a Parent-Teacher Conference	Attended a Class Event	Volunteered at School
Less than $5,000	67.0	68.3	49.8	27.0
$5,001–$10,000	63.8	67.4	49.6	24.4
$10,001–$15,000	67.4	66.9	60.3	29.9
$15,001–$20,000	69.1	67.4	55.8	26.8
$20,001–$25,000	69.0	68.7	58.5	29.2
$25,001–$30,000	72.0	69.2	61.7	33.0
$30,001–$35,000	79.0	69.1	68.8	41.6
$35,001–$40,000	78.9	72.8	69.6	41.7
$40,001–$50,000	80.7	73.9	72.8	45.3
$50,001–$75,000	83.9	72.2	75.0	49.1
More than $75,000	88.2	73.8	79.1	57.3

Source: National Center for Education Statistics (1999), Table 25.

---

[9]These efforts are being supported by state and district actions. For instance, following the
California Family-School Partnership Act of 1995, the California State Board of Education now
requires schools to push for parental involvement, even if it is simply encouraging parents to help
students with homework. Furthermore, some school districts are providing support organizations to
promote parent involvement. The San Francisco Unified School District, for example, opened a parent
and community involvement office in the 1996–1997 school year to help its 112 schools support
parent volunteer efforts (Schevitz, 1997).

[10]For research that reports patterns of involvement across school grades, on families with low
and high socioeconomic status, one- and two-parent homes, and schools' programs of partnership,
see Dauber and Epstein (1993), Dornbusch and Ritter (1988), Eccles (1996), Epstein and Lee (1995),
and Lareau (1989).

In addition to parents, local businesses provide important support to public schools. Local businesses tend to support schools in their own cities and within proximity to their business locations (Mamokhin, 2000). These businesses provide donations of items such as food, meeting spaces, and school supplies; serve as student mentors and tutors; and provide award and gift certificates to honor teachers and students.

Corporations are also key givers to public education.[11] They have the resources to both help finance school programs and act as advocates for specific policies at the national and local levels. Corporate involvement dates back to the nineteenth century when business leaders were extensively involved with the movement to set up universal common schools, and encouraged public schools to adapt business principles in how they operate (Timpane and McNeill, 1991). This support waned over the middle of the twentieth century, but has rebounded with an increase in school-business partnerships in recent decades (McGuire, 1990).

In addition, large philanthropic foundations, such as the Carnegie Corporation and the Ford Foundation, have been contributing significantly to public education since the late-1950s and continue to provide financial contributions today (Meade, 1991).[12] Other organizations such as community groups, colleges and universities, and alumni organizations have also been supported public schools in various ways.

A wide variety of community-based organizations, including YMCAs, boys clubs and girls clubs, chambers of commerce, the Boy Scouts and Girl Scouts, and rotary clubs, have provided time and in-kind resources to public schools.[13] Colleges and universities generally require education majors to spend time in schools and encourage younger students to visit college campuses. Service-learning, which involves integrating community service with academic curricula, has become more common on college campuses, and K–12 students and classrooms are the primary beneficiaries of college students' service activities (Gray et al., 1999). The range of service activities includes tutoring, mentoring,

---

[11]As we define it, the difference between local businesses and corporations is in the scope of their market: Local businesses serve the local market whereas corporations serve a much broader one.

[12]The largest single gift ever made to American public education is the Annenberg Challenge grant, funded by the Annenberg Foundation. Ambassador Walter Annenberg's $500 million, five-year challenge grant is designed to energize, support, and replicate successful school reform programs throughout the country. Los Angeles Unified School district and districts in surrounding Los Angeles County are recipients of a $53 million Annenberg challenge grant, to be matched one-for-one.

[13]For example, the Los Angeles Educational Partnership (LAEP) is a nonprofit organization working to support public education in the Los Angeles area. Since 1984, LAEP has invested more than $50 million in teacher development, school reform, and community services in Los Angeles–area schools and communities.

and other classroom support programs. Finally, school alumni associations have been forming across the nation to raise monetary support (Glass, 1995).

Channeling Giving Through School-Based Organizations and Individuals

Often, when a private individual or group gives to public education, it channels its contributions through a school or district-based organization. The prevalence of particular organizations in California schools and districts is displayed in Table 2.4.[14] Of these, PTAs are the most popular, not only in California but nationwide. Today, the national PTA organization has more than 6.5 million members in more than 26,000 local chapters throughout the country.

While PTAs are the most common school-based organization, they are certainly not the only ones. Other groups include Parent Teacher Organizations (PTOs) and booster clubs, which are generally not affiliated with a national organization. Whereas PTAs typically focus on national or state education issues and are service organizations in addition to being fund-raising organizations, PTOs and booster clubs essentially are just fund-raising organizations. Booster clubs often target their efforts toward one particular activity, such as an athletic team or club (for example, a marching band or chorus). These organizations typically serve an individual school rather than an entire district. Some schools have more than

Table 2.4
Organizations Channeling Private Resources in California

Category	Total	Description
PTAs	974	Teacher-parent groups that are members of the California Congress of Parents, Teachers, and Students, Inc.
Booster clubs	692	Groups that obtain private funding for school programs
LEFs	537	Community-based organizations, generally associated with districts, that raise private support
PTOs	328	Teacher-parent groups that are not members of the California Congress of Parents, Teachers, and Students, Inc.

Source: Brunner and Sonstelie, 1997.

---

[14]As a point of reference, in 1997, California had 1,060 school districts and 7,913 schools. The counts of PTAs, booster clubs, LEFs, and PTOs in the Brunner and Sonstelie (1997) research are not totals for the state. The IRS data that their research relied upon include only nonprofit organizations with relatively high levels of total monetary contributions. Therefore, the totals for the state are likely to be considerably higher than those shown in Table 2.4.

one of these organizations in operation. All are also typically run for parents, and use a range of methods for raising support—from special events to bake sales to mail solicitations.

A fourth type of organization that has only recently come into prominence is the local education foundation, or LEF.[15] LEFs are tax-exempt, nonprofit, community-based organizations; they can be started by active parents or by district staff who solicit parent or community member involvement to run the foundation.[16]

As opposed to PTAs, PTOs, and booster clubs, LEFs typically operate at the district level, but they are independent of the school districts they serve. A common model for a LEF consists of a single foundation that serves all the schools in one district. On the other hand, some LEFs and the districts they serve allow individual schools to form their own foundations. Another model is a single foundation that serves several districts in a region.

Foundations are often sophisticated entities with board members and directors, and several steering committees that concentrate on such issues as advertising, public relations, and fund-raising strategies. Because of their structure and position outside the public school system, LEFs can write grants, secure donations of services or funds, mount programs, and make payments faster than other traditional organizations or the schools themselves.

Some foundations concern themselves mainly with fund-raising while others focus more heavily on bringing about systemic reform in schools, working in areas such as school governance, educational leadership, curriculum, and assessment of educational programs. Foundations tend to focus on bigger gifts than the PTAs or clubs; therefore, they pursue a smaller number of donors giving larger amounts of money (Addonizio, 1999).[17] Thus, successful LEFs can raise a signifi-

---

[15]Although the largest growth of these foundations occurred after 1989, the boom started in the early 1980s in some states that had newly approved property tax limitation measures (Merz and Frankel, 1995; Brunner and Sonstelie, 1997; Addonizio, 1999). The growth of LEFs appears to be particularly prominent in states that have instituted tax limitation policies. Soon after the 1978 passage of Proposition 13 in California, for example, the number of LEFs doubled in the state—from 22 in 1978 to 46 in 1980. California is widely believed to have the most LEFs, with a total of 537 LEFs in 1995, up from 204 in 1985 and 30 in 1979 (Brunner and Sonstelie, 1997). The lack of a nationwide LEF clearinghouse makes it nearly impossible to ascertain an accurate national number of such foundations. However, de Luna (1998) estimates that there are more than 2,000 LEFs nationwide.

[16]There are three primary advantages to qualifying as a tax-exempt organization under section 501(c)(3) of the Internal Revenue Code. First, such an organization is normally exempt from federal income taxes. Second, contributions to a 501(c)(3) organization usually result in a tax deduction for the donor. And, finally, such an organization is in a position to attract grants from other tax-exempt organizations (Merz and Frankel, 1995).

[17]In response to the growth in LEFs, associations have formed in various states to assist foundations. In California, for example, the California Consortium of Education Foundations (CCEF) was formed as a way to share ideas among LEFs in the state and provide advice on forming and maintaining a foundation. The CCEF acts as a unified voice for the local education foundations across a state. In addition, 84 foundations in 26 states and the District of Columbia belong to the Public

16

cant amount of funds. For example, a Pasadena, California, LEF raised $1 million in donations and $6 million in grants in 2000 for Pasadena public schools (Fox, 2001).[18]

In addition to these organizations, there are individuals at both the school and district level who are instrumental in channeling private resources to public schools. Recent news articles suggest that the fund-raising role of school and district leaders has taken on greater importance over time. A good superintendent, much like a good university president, goes out and raises money for the district (Richardson, 1994). Similar stories are heard at the school level. The principal of a high school in Inglewood, California, for example, reported using personal contacts to obtain more than $200,000 in gifts and grants for her school over three years (Richardson, 1994).

Mechanisms for Attracting Private Support

Public schools and school district organizations and individuals use a variety of mechanisms to attract resources from private givers. Traditionally, the basis for attracting private monetary resources has been fund-raising events. Fund-raisers run the gamut from product sales to special events such as raffles, auctions, and dinner dances. Fund-raising is such a staple at public schools that it has spawned an entire industry that does nothing but supply products for fund-raisers (for example, wrapping paper and candy).

Two other popular methods of attracting private support are mass mailings and phone solicitations. At San Pedro High School in California, for example, the school librarian sent out more than 2,000 letters to companies and organizations asking them to donate their used computer equipment—the campaign resulted in the donation of 19 computers (Richardson, 1994). The Lake Oswego School District Foundation in Oregon relies primarily on "phonathons" to raise money. In the spring of 1995, the school district collected about $100,000 over a two-night effort during which 70 volunteers telephoned 5,000 households (de Luna, 1998). While fund-raising for schools is not a new idea, there is the sense that it has

---

Education Network (PEN). The main focus of foundations associated with PEN is to bring about systemic reform in schools and work in policy areas (de Luna, 1998).

[18]The success of these foundations has raised issues regarding equity. In Los Angeles County, one school district raised as much as $400 per pupil, while other school districts raised nothing at all (Fox, 2001). Several recent research efforts (Merz and Frankel, 1995; Brunner and Sonstelie, 1997; Addonizio, 1999) conclude that foundation contributions constitute a small percentage of revenue in all but a handful of schools, and provide very small amounts of money compared when compared with school district budgets. Therefore, they have little effect on the per-pupil amounts available to districts. Other research (Crampton and Bauman, 1998) suggests that entrepreneurship did have a disequalizing impact on intradistrict and interdistrict fiscal equity.

become more intense, varied, widespread, and profitable over the past decade or so (Walker, 1999).

Although product sales, one-time events, and mail and phone solicitation fund-raisers are important, the literature suggests that personal contacts and relationship building are key to raising support in a more meaningful and sustained way (Mamokhin, 2000). Personal contacts allow the person channeling the private resources an "in" with the prospective private giver. Relationship building can involve keeping the giver up to date on school activities and making the giver feel like a partner by ensuring that the relationship is mutually beneficial to both the giver and receiver.

Another more-recent trend involves districts and schools soliciting the services of paid consultants to help them establish local education foundations and advise them on innovative ways to raise private support (Mathews, 1995).[19] This marks a growing intensity and sophistication with which schools and districts are approaching private giving.

Types of Private Giving

The fund-raising efforts described in the previous section lead to both in-kind and monetary private resources for public schools and districts. However, data on the type and quantity of giving are not systematically collected at either the school or district level. Furthermore, in-kind support is inherently harder to quantify than is monetary support—it is more difficult to assign value to someone's time than to an amount written on a check. In this section, we highlight what is currently known about these two major types of support. Whereas one can find many examples of in-kind support in the literature, it is difficult to know the relative size of in-kind versus monetary support and the relative importance of each to public schools.[20]

---

[19]One consulting firm that helps start up educational foundations reports having 300 public school clients. This is clearly a small percentage of the overall number of schools in the United States, but it will be interesting to see if the number of schools seeking help and the number of consultants increase over time.

[20]Often, one kind of private support can lead to other kinds of private support. For example, Timpane and McNeill (1991) describe the unique stages of school-business relationships with different types of support at each stage. These relationships often begin as helping-hand relationships in which businesses provide tangible goods and services to schools (such as equipment, tutors, speakers, or special materials). After that, businesses may get involved in programmatic initiatives in an attempt to bring positive change to improve one particular school or program. Later on, businesses may form compacts and collaborative efforts that provide single community-wide umbrellas under which a wide range of school-business and school-community activities exist and, in one way or another, pressure for district-wide school reforms. At the final stage, business leaders and organizations get involved in policy changes and become active participants in developing a vast array of new policies, especially at the state level.

In-Kind Support

A variety of private givers—for example, parents, businesses, and community members—volunteer their time in public schools. Volunteer contributions cover a wide spectrum of support, such as volunteer time for tutoring, health services, office support, school governance, and fund-raising. Parent volunteer time in particular is critical to schools because parents have a stronger connection with schools than do other community members. Parents often volunteer in their own children's classrooms, sit on governance councils, and help organize and run fund-raising activities. For example, when Orange County, California, had a budgetary crisis and declared bankruptcy, the schools asked parents to help meet the shortfall in the budget by volunteering their time (Loar and Bean, 1994). The president of the Irvine PTA in Orange Country estimated that during the 1994–1995 school year, more than 280,000 hours of personal time were volunteered by parents who cleaned, painted, stuffed envelopes, tutored, and even taught (Graham, 1995).

Businesspeople also frequently volunteer their time in addition to providing material donations (Mamokhin, 2000). By all indications, the most widespread and popular type of relationship between businesses and schools is the so-called helping-hand relationship. Businesses provide resources that the schools would have difficulty securing on their own, such as guest speakers, computers and other equipment, volunteer time given by their employees, and mini-grants to teachers.

Seventeen percent of the nation's schools reported being part of business-school partnerships in 1984; this number grew to 40 percent in the early 1990s (Timpane and McNeill, 1991). In total, there are more than 140,000 partnerships in 30,000 public elementary and secondary schools across the nation. Small-business firms sponsor about 40 percent of the partnerships, while medium-size and larger firms each support roughly 30 percent.

A wide variety of business-school partnership models exists. A program in Prince Georges County, Maryland, for example, has been established to create partnerships between business leaders and school personnel. When county public school administrators needed help resolving some problems—from streamlining the bus system, to repairing aging buildings, to tracking down job candidates—school officials sought help from chief executives at successful businesses in the area. The businesses responded and created a program called Corporate Partnership on Managerial Excellence. Businesspeople paired with school administrators to teach the administrators skills that businesses routinely use to solve problems. For example, personnel experts worked with school human resource workers, construction professionals worked with construction division managers, and transportation professionals worked with school administrators to help overhaul their transportation division (Thomas-Lester, 2000).

In another example of business-school partnerships, virtually all districts in the South Bay in Los Angeles County solicit and receive contributions from the area's major aerospace, automobile, computer, and oil companies. For example, the Mattel Alumni Association offers a popular business education course at La Tijera School in Inglewood. The Inglewood Unified School District estimates that if it had to pay for the program, the district would need about $60,000 a year for the hours of labor and materials required for the class (Richardson, 1994).

Community-based organizations are also big givers of in-kind support, particularly in the areas of student and family support services, after-school programs, and enrichment programs. For example, some hospitals establish clinics at their local schools, providing nursing services, immunizations, and education programs to students and their families. Some community organizations provide family services such as parent education classes or English language classes. In addition, a variety of organizations, such as the YMCA and Boys Clubs and Girls Clubs, provide after-school programs. Further, community-based organizations often provide volunteer personnel for enrichment programs, along with related instructional materials.

Monetary Support

Private monetary support to public schools comes in many forms, including donations, percentages of product sales, scholarships, paid endorsements, user fees, and leasing of school facilities. Donations are a relatively straightforward type of support; they can be given to support a particular program or as flexible donations for use as the school sees fit. A wide variety of givers may make monetary donations to a school, including parents, corporations, philanthropic foundations, and city governments.

National and state databases generally do not detail the types and amounts of private monetary giving. When the data sets do account for financial donations, those donations are generally lumped together under a category called "other revenues." For instance, California Department of Education (CDE) data include revenue sources by school district, including property taxes, supplemental taxes, valorem taxes, interest income, and a category called "all other local revenue." The amount in the "all other" category is a lump-sum value with no description of the sources. As a result, it is impossible to track financial donations, let alone in-kind gifts.

Other researchers, including Brunner and Sonstelie (1997), have sought IRS data along with other data sets, including the Registry of Charitable Trusts located in Sacramento, which tracks nonprofit organizations. Through an arduous process, these data sets can be used to identify particular organizations, such as PTAs and LEFs, that are associated with schools and districts. Again, the data offer very limited information about the scope and quantity of both monetary and in-kind contributions to schools.[21]

Another type of monetary support worth noting results from schools receiving a percentage of sales from businesses. So-called *scrip* programs, for example, allow individuals to contribute to schools by purchasing scrip certificates for goods that they would normally buy. Scrip certificates are sold at a slight discount to schools and the schools make money by reselling the certificates at full value to parents and other supporters. Scrip is available from a variety of businesses selling everything from groceries, clothes, and restaurant meals, to toys, flowers, and airline tickets. Parents at Monterey Hills Elementary School in South Pasadena, California, for example, raised about $10,000 annually buying scrip from supermarkets and smaller retail chains. Businesses benefit because they attract customers, and also because they are paid in advance, providing ready cash before goods and services are delivered (Ellingwood and Hong, 1998).

Another area of private monetary support comes in the form of paid endorsements and advertising revenue. A Colorado Springs, Colorado, school district is believed to be the first in the nation to allow commercial advertising on school walls, athletic uniforms, newsletters, district reports, maps, stadium walls, and buses. In the past, securing corporate sponsors for state high school athletic tournaments was not unusual. Presently, school districts in several states are active in seeking corporate sponsorship for academic and extracurricular activities, in addition to athletic events.

Funds generated from advertising can be substantial. In Chula Vista, south of San Diego, California, the Sweetwater Union High School District signed an exclusive deal with the Pepsi-Cola Company that will bring in at least $4.45 million to the district's 20 schools over the next ten years. The money will pay for technology, library books, intramural sports, music programs, and school-to-career programs (Groves, 1999).

---

[21]In our study, we do not analyze these data sets. However, we may do so in future projects to help identify private givers to public schools.

Schools generated an estimated $750 million in revenue from vending machines in 1997, according to the trade journal *Vending Times.* However, paid endorsements and advertising revenue in public schools are controversial. One district has taken a stand against commercialism in public schools, declaring that its city's schoolchildren are "not for sale"—the San Francisco school board approved a trend-bucking policy seeking to limit commercial advertising and paid endorsements in the city's public schools (Groves, 1999). Currently, 19 states have created statutes or regulations that address commercial activities within schools (GAO, 2000).

In addition, United States Senator Patrick Leahy of Vermont has announced that he will introduce legislation "that would allow the federal government to more tightly restrict soft drink sales in schools" (Kaufman, 2001). The Coca-Cola Company has acknowledged critics' concerns and is planning to announce a new policy to discourage its bottlers from signing exclusivity agreements with schools (Kaufman, 2001). The new policy is a reaction to concerns about both the commercialization of schools and the health of school children. PepsiCo has said that it will follow Coca-Cola's lead.

Use of Private Monetary Giving

Private monetary giving supports a wide range of activities that tend to fall into three main categories: current operations, technology, and capital improvements. Most monetary giving, except for the generally small amount of funds coming from percentages of product sales, tends to be targeted to particular functions or goals.

Private dollars devoted to current operations support a variety of activities that affect the day-to-day operation of a school or district. One use of private dollars is for the professional development of teachers and administrators. A recent study (Useem, 1999) found that professional development efforts were the activities most frequently targeted by LEFs. All 17 of the LEFs that Useem studied had programs that supported the training of teachers, administrators, or other school personnel. Learning opportunities provided to staff included training on particular content areas, such as mathematics or science; assistance with curriculum development; mini-grants for individual teacher enrichment; leadership development; new teacher workforce development; and technology training.

How private monies are spent on current operations varies from site to site and often depends on the amount each site is able to raise. Donations may be used to fund enrichment programs, such as a special arts program or a substance abuse prevention program, or the purchase of instructional materials, such as workbooks or curriculum guides, or school supplies and equipment, such as paper or VCRs. Private dollars frequently enable teachers to try out creative classroom teaching projects, especially at those schools and districts with smaller fund-raising capacities.

At the other end of the money-collecting spectrum are those districts and schools that bring in enough private funding to support teaching positions. A recent national study of local education foundations found that LEFs that raise $10,000 or less annually usually spend their funds on mini-grants and scholarships (Merz and Frankel, 1995). Foundations that collect from $20,000 to $50,000 annually tend to spend the money on curriculum enrichment programs, teacher training, and teaching resources, and those that bring in more than $100,000 annually often pay for teaching positions. In addition, school- and district-based fund-raising entities that concentrate their efforts on reforming education tend to spend their donations on such activities as professional development, policy development, public relations, and the promotion of school-business partnerships (de Luna, 1998).

Other uses of private dollars include investments in technology and capital improvements. Of the 17 LEFs recently studied by Useem (1999), a majority administered programs that integrated computer-based technologies into various aspects of school reform. The projects raised money for technology efforts, encouraged voters to support expenditures for technology, recruited volunteers to assist schools with technology, provided training to school constituencies, and created on-line services and Internet home pages with educational and social service resources and databases.

In addition, schools and school districts use private dollars for a variety of building improvements. A GAO study (1995) documents the poor state of American public school facilities. Some schools and districts are responding by seeking private support to improve the physical condition of the schools. Although large-scale capital projects are usually beyond the means of private support, private support is nevertheless used for a variety of school building safety, enhancement, and beautification projects (Anderson, 1997; Warchol, 1997).

Limitations of Study Research

Partly due to the dearth of local, state, and federal data on private giving, we currently do not have a comprehensive and systematic picture of private support to public schools and districts. Newspaper accounts of private giving provide anecdotal evidence on the "who, what, and how" of private support to public education. That evidence suggests that a wide range of school and district-based organizations are using a variety of mechanisms to channel monetary and in-kind support to public education from a variety of private givers. In addition, it is likely that different types of communities call on different types of private monetary and in-kind resources.

Recent research literature on private support of public education largely examines private monetary support of education, particularly that from LEFs. This is not surprising given that monetary support is relatively easy to document compared with in-kind support. And, raising monetary support through LEFs is a recent and growing phenomenon. While LEFs are clearly an important component of private support, they do not present a complete picture of private support available to public education. Furthermore, to the extent that schools or districts obtain monetary support, we do not currently have an understanding of how the funds are distributed and for what purposes. These limitations are addressed throughout this report.

3. Research Methodology

To answer our "who, how, and what" questions regarding private giving to public schools, we selected a sample of schools and districts that represent[1] the diversity of the student population and communities within Los Angeles County. Our site visits gave us the opportunity to question school and school district personnel about their fund-raising activities. Our belief was that we could learn more from personal interviews than from the data that currently exist. This type of research methodology is particularly well suited to exploratory analysis because it allows a researcher to ask more open-ended questions and develop hypotheses that can be studied in greater depth in future research.

In this chapter, we describe our process for choosing the sample and conducting interviews with school and district personnel. The results of our analysis will not only help us develop hypotheses for future research, but also build a foundation for survey instrument development and provide descriptive details of private giving to public schools.

District and School Selection

Los Angeles County is one of the most heavily populated and diverse counties in the United States. Similarly, the school districts within the county are diverse, in both their size and demographics. In total, there are more than 1.6 million students in close to 1,700 schools in 83 districts in Los Angeles County. Among those districts is the second-largest one in the United States—the Los Angeles Unified School District (LAUSD). In the 1998–1999 school year, LAUSD had close to 700,000 students and a total annual budget of $4.27 billion. In contrast, both by size and budget, Gorman Elementary School District in Los Angeles County had at the time of our study just over 100 students and a budget of just $1.1 million.

In addition to their differences in size, districts within Los Angeles County are racially/ethnically and socioeconomically diverse. However, districts and schools are often highly segregated across demographic characteristics. In nearly half the districts, more than 70 percent of the student population is in a single

---

[1]In this chapter, we use the words "represent" and "representative" to mean "reflects" or "is similar to." Because the districts and schools were not randomly selected, the sample is not "representative" in the statistical sense of the word, and therefore we cannot draw conclusions about the larger population of schools and districts.

racial/ethnic group, and in some individual schools the entire student population is composed of a single racial/ethnic group. Similarly, participants in the federally funded Free and Reduced Price Lunch Program, whose eligibility is based on income, represent nearly 100 percent the student population in a few districts, while in other districts these students represent as little as 2 percent of the student population.

The diversity of Los Angeles County is evident in the different characteristics of its various regions. The county covers more than 4,000 square miles with distinctive ethnic, cultural, and business pockets, which ultimately leads to unique communities with their own sense of identity. These differences also may lead to differing patterns in private giving. A large district with a high percentage of minority students in the southern part of the county may have a very different level of parental and community involvement, and may use different strategies to gain private support, than would a small district with a small percentage of minorities in the northern part of the county.

District Selection

In selecting districts to visit, we attempted to create a sample with a degree of diversity as close as possible to that of Los Angeles County as a whole so that we could identify the full range of activities taking place in the region. We also wanted to examine whether private giving varied across schools and districts depending on their particular characteristics, including size, quality of education, socioeconomic status, and demographics. Therefore, to create our sample, districts were stratified by geographic area, and by educational, socioeconomic, and demographic indicators. Indicators included test scores,[2] district size, percentage of Hispanic students, percentage of African-American students, percentage of white students, and percentage of Free and Reduced Price Lunch Program participants.[3]

The geographic areas of the sample included San Fernando Valley/North Los Angeles, West Los Angeles, East Los Angeles, Central Los Angeles, South Los Angeles, and the South Bay beach communities. Using these six regions, we selected one district per geographic area and one to two schools per district. In total, ten schools were selected. More specifically, two schools per district were

---

[2]The indicator is based on the performance of individual pupils on the Standardized Testing and Reporting (STAR) content area tests, as measured through national percentile rankings (NPRs). STAR program test scores are on a scale of 200 to 1,000.

[3]The data on school and district characteristics in Los Angeles County come from the National Center for Education Statistics' (NCES) Common Core Data (CCD) and CDE data files. Specifically, CCD data files provided financial and demographic data and CDE data provided test score results.

selected from the San Fernando Valley/North Los Angeles, West Los Angeles, Central Los Angeles, and South Los Angeles areas. One school per district was selected from the East Los Angeles and South Bay beach areas.[4]

Table 3.1 highlights the mean district and student characteristics of the selected districts relative to the mean district and student characteristics of the county as a whole, and Table 3.2 highlights the respective quartile ranking of the selected districts for each of these same characteristics.[5]

As Table 3.1 shows, on average, the selected districts are larger than the average Los Angeles County district. The districts selected for our sample have a slightly higher percentage of African-American students, a significantly higher percentage of white students, and a smaller percentage of Hispanic and free lunch program students, while their test scores are near the county mean.

Table 3.2 displays the specific quartile (1 through 4) into which each of six sample districts falls relative to the rest of the county. A district with a rank of 1 is in the highest quartile of that characteristic whereas a district with a rank of 4 is in the lowest quartile. Districts with a rank of 2 or 3 are in the second or third quartiles, respectively, and we characterize these as more-average districts.

Table 3.2 shows that our sample has four relatively large districts, one average-size district, and one small district. This suggests that we over-sampled large districts.[6] As for the percentage of white, African-American, and Hispanic students, the sample is fairly comparable to the county's percentages, with four average-

Table 3.1

Comparison of Selected School Districts Relative to Los Angeles County as a Whole (Mean Characteristics)

	Total Students	Percentage White	Percentage African-American	Percentage Hispanic	Percentage of Free Lunch Program Participants	Test Scores
County	19,891	19.8	11.4	58.6	61.3	641
Selected sample	26,052	34.8	12.8	38.6	42.7	626

---

[4]We visited only one school in these districts because the South Bay Beach District is small and the East Los Angeles district had only one school that had substantial private interaction.

[5]Because we have ensured anonymity to our participating schools and districts, we are not including the districts' names. Rather, we will refer to them by their geographic areas.

[6]This overrepresentation is partially the result of having multiple criteria for selecting districts—it is difficult to achieve a representative sample when trying to sample across a number of criteria.

Table 3.2

Quartile Ranking of Selected Districts for Key Characteristics

District	Total Students	Percentage White	Percentage African-American	Percentage Hispanic	Percentage of Free Lunch Program Participants	Test Scores
A	1	3	3	1	1	4
B	1	2	3	2	3	2
C	1	4	1	2	1	4
D	1	4	1	3	2	3
E	4	1	3	4	4	1
F	2	2	2	3	4	1

size districts for African-Americans and Hispanics and three average-size districts for whites.

Two districts have a large percentage of African-American students, and one district has a large percentage of Hispanics. Two districts have a small percentage of white students and one district has a small percentage of Hispanic students. In terms of poverty levels and student achievement, as measured by the percentage of Free Lunch program participants and standardized test scores, the sample, with its two average, two high-ranking, and two low-ranking districts, resembles the county overall. Therefore, we believe that our sample reflects the county as a whole (with the exception of the overrepresentation of large districts).

In each district, we first contacted the superintendent's office to get permission to include the district in our study. A few districts declined to participate and were replaced by districts with similar demographics. One district refused because district personnel said the district did not engage in any fund-raising efforts, although it did have a very successful education foundation. A second district declined without offering an explanation. In the districts that agreed to participate, we interviewed either the superintendent or members of the superintendent's staff responsible for private giving. In two of those districts, we met with the superintendent; in the other four districts, we met with staff members responsible for private giving. Staff members typically had titles that included the words "Business Partnerships" or "Community Partnerships."

School Selection

Part of the overall goal of this report is to provide information to schools and school districts about the kinds of private-giving partnerships that have been developed in various communities and the mechanisms used to attract private resources. Therefore, we wanted a sample of schools that was not selected at random; instead, we wanted a selection that would provide useful information to other schools in developing their own partnerships.

To select the schools, we asked district-level staff to identify one or two elementary schools in the district considered to be good examples in terms of raising private support. In four of the six districts, we visited two schools. In those cases, we asked district staff to designate one low-income and one high-income school for our interview, so that the lessons learned would be relevant to a range of schools. In the other two districts, we asked district staff to designate the school most exemplary of being successful at attracting private giving, regardless of economic standing. We then contacted those schools to set up meetings with the schools' principals. One school in the original sample never responded to our inquiry, so the district office provided us with a backup recommendation.

Table 3.3 displays the total number of students; percentage of students who are African-American, Hispanic or white; percentage of students with free lunch program participation; and the school mean test score for each of the selected schools. Comparing the mean and median of the sample characteristics of the schools with the characteristics of the districts suggests that our school sample is overrepresented by schools with high averages of African-American and Hispanic students, and students participating in the free lunch program. However, the mean test scores for all schools in the sample are very similar to the districts' test scores as a whole.

Therefore, readers should keep these overrepresentations in mind when examining our results. Despite these differences with the districts, our sample of schools does include a wide array of school characteristics, with some schools having very low percentages of African-American, Hispanic, and free lunch program students and other schools having relatively high percentages of such students. In addition, school size and test score outcomes also vary widely among schools.

While we wanted a representative sample, our selection process was more purposive than random; therefore, one should be cautious when drawing conclusions from our results. In the final section of this chapter, we discuss in more detail the limitations and caveats associated with the sample.

In addition to the district and school site visits, we conducted phone interviews with representatives from the local education foundations in three of the six sample districts. We received no response from one district foundation, and the other two districts have no foundations associated with them (although one of those two districts is currently in the process of establishing a LEF).

Table 3.3

Sample Schools Description

District/School	Total Students	Percentage White	Percentage African-American	Percentage Hispanic	Percentage of Free Lunch Program Participants	Test Scores
District A						
School A	660	5	0	95	90	590
District B						
School B	720	40	0	50	60	660
School C	800	5	60	20	15	640
District C						
School D	440	0	70	30	100	610
School E	970	0	30	70	100	610
District D						
School F	1130	5	25	40	80	620
School G	820	5	20	70	100	620
District E						
School H	630	80	0	5	5	660
District F						
School I	360	45	10	40	55	620
School J	830	80	0	10	5	660
Sample Average	735.6	26.6	21.9	42.6	60.1	629
Sample Median	758.5	5.4	14.7	38.2	68.6	620

Note: The total student numbers and test scores have been rounded to the nearest 10 and the columns indicating race or free lunch program participation have been rounded to the nearest 5 to protect the identity of the schools.

Interview Topics

We developed separate protocols for the three sets of interviews (district, school, and LEF), although similar topics were addressed in each of them (Appendices A, B, and C list the interview protocols). Having three different protocols enabled us to explore the same topics from multiple perspectives. The interviews covered a range of topics that reflected our research questions:

- How do the districts, schools, and foundations raise support, whether monetary, in-kind material donations, or volunteer time?
- Who contributes, what do they contribute, and how much do they contribute?
- How are the resources allocated across each district and within the schools?
- What types of programs are supported?

In addition to questions about their individual efforts, we were interested in the interplay between the various entities, so we asked general questions about the relationships between each district and its foundation and schools, and specifically about the amount of support provided by the district and foundation to the schools.

During the district-level site visits, we also asked that the respondents complete a form regarding the district's five largest private gifts. The form asked for information such as the amount, giver, and dollar value of the gift; time frame of the gift giving; and use of the gift. Four of the districts returned completed forms. In addition, we obtained written documents, including annual reports, from some of the sites, and obtained newsletters and copies of mail solicitations used to collect donations from other sites.

Analysis

The site visits were conducted between August 2000 and January 2001, with two or three RAND researchers visiting each site. Following each visit, the researchers prepared notes documenting the interview. After all the visits were completed, the team met as a group to review the field notes and identify patterns and themes.

We developed a matrix, using as its basis the major research questions, and then used the matrix to record the results of each site visit. The matrix categories are as follows: private givers; school or district-based entity channeling private resources; mechanism to attract private resources; types of private giving; and use of private monetary giving.

Within each category, we developed a comprehensive list of different examples; for instance, in the category of private givers, the list of examples includes parents, local businesses, and philanthropic foundations, to name just a few. These examples were derived from an extensive literature review (as outlined in Chapter 2), the site visits themselves, and from interviews with LEFs and other individuals. We then reviewed the notes on each site to determine whether we saw evidence of each example at a particular site. Data from the forms that district staff filled out were also used in completing the matrix results.

Other Interviews

In addition to the site visits and foundation interviews, we also interviewed several experts in the field of private giving to public schools. The expertise of these individuals covered a range of topic areas, including business partnerships, fund-raising, and education foundation development. We did not follow a standard protocol for these interviews, but rather engaged in somewhat unstructured conversations. These interviews supplemented the district, school, and foundation interviews, and provided a slightly different perspective on several of our research questions.

Data Limitations

As we noted earlier, this research project was designed to serve as a pilot study for examining how public schools raise support from private sources. As a pilot study, it was necessarily limited in scope.

The most-profound limitation in our study, due to the scope of the research, was our inability to provide information concerning the dollar value of private monetary and in-kind contributions. In future studies, this issue hopefully can be addressed with more-probing questions.

Another major limitation in our analysis was sample size. By including only ten schools and six districts in Los Angeles County, our analysis may not capture all facets of private support. The sample size also restricts our ability to gain statistically significant differences among the school types, givers, gifts, and other elements of the study. In addition, we included only elementary schools in our sample; middle and high schools may show different patterns of private giving.

Another limitation is that we purposely selected a sample of elementary schools that had successful programs for attracting private giving.[7] Through our study, we wanted to be able to identify and describe successful strategies for gaining private support. Because of this sample-selection strategy, our sample may not demonstrate every successful means of raising private support.

Finally, our analysis is limited in that we interviewed only school, district, and foundation staff, and did not seek input from donors. Thus, our conclusions are drawn solely from the schools' and districts' perspective.[8]

---

[7]However, we found that two of the schools had almost no involvement from parents, businesses, or the community.

[8]In addition, school officials may not have an incentive to provide information on the total value of private giving. Crampton and Bauman (1998) suggested that schools might not disclose the full value of private giving because of certain equity implications. Schools receiving a substantial amount of private gifts may be afraid that state or district monetary support will decrease because of these gifts.

Despite these limitations, we believe our analysis provides many lessons to be learned that can be informative to both district and school-level personnel and policymakers. In the next chapter, we provide results from our analysis.

4. The Who, How, and What of Private Giving

As we've noted in this report, our review of the literature on private giving to public schools raised several questions on who the private givers are, how schools and districts attract private support, and what type of support they get and how that support is used. We sought answers to these questions through site visits to six school districts in Los Angeles County and ten schools within those districts.

To document our findings, we developed a matrix of private giving, displayed in Table 4.1. The content of the matrix was developed first through our review of the literature,[1] and then supplemented with data we gathered during our site visits. This matrix presents a useful framework for examining the various dimensions of private giving.

Table 4.1 demonstrates the potential paths that resources might follow as they move from private givers to eventual use by districts and schools. Specifically, both monetary and in-kind resources flow from private givers through various entities that attract donations through a variety of mechanisms. In turn, private giving may take a variety of forms and be used for diverse purposes.

The matrix serves as the framework for our discussion of the results of our study. The beginning sections in this chapter correspond to the column headings in the Table 4.1 matrix. We explore the *how*, *why*, and *what* of private giving from the perspective of the district staff members and school principals whom we interviewed. We note the frequency of each type of private giving and describe how these resources are used at both the district and school level.

We also discuss differences across schools and districts to the extent that private giving appears to be related to school and district socioeconomic status, as measured by participation in the federally funded Free and Reduced Price Lunch Program.[2]

---

[1]See Appendix E for additional details on the sources for each of the items included in the matrix.

[2]We also examined patterns of private involvement by district and school size, racial/ethnic makeup, and the tenure of superintendents and principals. In general, no clear patterns were revealed through these analyses.

Table 4.1

Matrix of Private Giving to Public Schools

Private Givers	Entity Channeling Private Resources	Mechanisms to Attract Private Resources	Types of Private Giving		Use of Private Monetary Giving	
			IN-KIND	**MONETARY**	**Current Operations**	**Technology**
Advocacy groups	Advisory board	Grant applications	**Volunteer time**	Donation	Athletics	Computers/software
Alumni	Booster club	High-profile speakers/hosts	Administrative	Endorsements/advertising revenue	Classroom teachers	**Capital Improvements**
City governments	District staff	K–12 higher-education partnerships	After-school programs	Leasing of facilities and services	Curriculum enrichment programs	Building additions
Colleges/universities	LEF	Leasing of school facilities	Classroom support	Paid membership dues	Early childhood education	Building enhancement
Community-based organizations	Other school-based club/association	Link with city planning	Enrichment programs	Percentage of product sales	Health services	Furniture
Community members	Principal	Local and national presentations	Family services	Scholarships	Instructional materials	Heating/air-conditioning
Corporations	PTA	Local newspaper advertising	School facilities	User fees	Other staff salaries	Playground equipment
Local businesses	PTO	Mail solicitation	School/district promotion	Wills/bequests	Parent education programs	School beautification
Other public agencies	School-site/leadership council	Participation in scrip or Web site programs	Staff training		Professional development	Sports facilities
Parents	Superintendent	Peer pressure	Student instruction		Promotion of school/business partnerships	
Philanthropic foundations		Personal contact/relationship building	Student mentoring		Salary enhancement or stipends for existing teachers	
Professionals associations		Phone solicitation	Student support services		School maintenance	
Students		Product sales	Student tutoring		School supplies/equipment	
		Professional fund-raiser	**Material Donations**		Special events	
		School-business partnerships	Awards/gift certificates		Student supplies	
		Special events	Equipment		Student transportation	
			Food		Teacher aides	
			Instructional materials			
			Off-site facilities for events			
			School supplies			
			Student/family supplies			
			Technology			

Who Are the Private Givers?

Private givers to public education include parents, businesses, philanthropic foundations, nonprofit organizations, community members, colleges and universities, and alumni. Each private giver often provides a variety of private support, both monetary and in-kind. In addition, the types of private support may change as the private giver–public school relationship develops over time.

Table 4.2 (which corresponds to the first column in Table 4.1) lists the private givers to the six districts and ten schools we visited in this pilot study. The left-hand column lists the private givers to the schools; the number of respondents who mentioned receiving support from each particular type of giver is shown in parentheses. The right-hand column shows the corresponding information at the district level.

At the School Level

Although parental involvement was the most common form of "giving" at the school level, other contributors also played a significant role in providing support to schools. A majority of schools relied on parents, local businesses, corporations, and community-based organizations for support. Although the level of support from each of these givers varied from school to school, as discussed later in this chapter, these four types of private givers played a role in most of the schools we studied.

Table 4.2

Private Givers in School and District Sample

Schools	Districts
Parents (10)	Corporations (6)
Local businesses (8)	Local businesses (6)
Community-based organizations (6)	Colleges/universities (4)
Corporations (6)	Community-based organizations (4)
City government (3)	Community members (4)
Community members (3)	Parents (4)
Philanthropic foundations (3)	City government (3)
Professional associations (3)	Philanthropic foundations (3)
Students (3)	Other public agencies (1)
Advocacy groups (2)	Professional associations (1)
Alumni (1)	Advocacy groups (0)
Colleges/universities (1)	Alumni (0)
Other public agencies (1)	Students (0)

Although they are a less-prevalent presence *across* schools, students, philanthropic foundations, community members, professional associations, and city governments are givers (and often donate gifts of significant size) to 25 to 50 percent of the sample schools. For example, two schools had sizable arts programs funded by their city governments. In addition, some other schools received significant monetary contributions from community members to improve school facilities. At another school, a program was developed in which older students (as well as parents and school staff) served as tutors for younger students. In contrast, colleges and universities did *not* play an active role in our sample schools—they were mentioned by only one school. This is surprising given that most of the schools that we visited had colleges or universities nearby. Some of the schools mentioned that at one time they had some loose connections with the local colleges and universities, but those relationships had not continued.

At the District Level

Our sample districts attracted support from many of the same private givers as the sample schools, although the size of those contributions differed, as discussed later. The most commonly reported types of private givers to districts were local businesses and corporations; all six of our districts reported receiving resources from these two groups. Community members were also active givers to several of our districts (serving on advisory boards or sponsoring events).

Although many of the school districts reported that parents were involved at the district level, either by volunteering their time or donating money, this type of support was far more prevalent and extensive at the school level. In contrast, colleges and universities played a considerably greater role at the district level as compared with at the school level.

Overall, school districts tended to attract resources from larger and more-organized groups, such as corporations, local businesses, and colleges and universities, as opposed to individuals and smaller groups and associations, which were the typical givers at the school level.

School-Based and District-Based Entities Channeling Private Resources

Our review of the literature suggested that private givers generally contribute their in-kind and monetary support through some organization or individual. These organizations and individuals use a variety of mechanisms, as outlined later, to attract private support to the district and/or school.

Table 4.3 lists the various entities that channel private resources to the ten schools and six districts in our sample. The number in parentheses following each entry indicates the number of schools or districts that mentioned receiving support through that entity.

At the School Level

At all of the sample schools, the principal was involved to some degree in attracting private resources to each school. In general, it was the principal who took the lead in developing relationships and promoting communication efforts with the community at large and other private sponsors. In addition, the principal was often the sole connection a school had with business and community sponsors.

The majority of schools also enlisted PTAs and LEFs to attract private support. PTAs raised private monetary support through a variety of fund-raisers and other activities and were key players in securing in-kind, volunteer types of support. Although seven schools cited the existence of a district LEF, only one school regarded the LEF as a significant player in attracting private support. For most schools, the LEF played a periphery role, such as getting uniforms donated to needy students or providing small teaching grants (such as monies used to implement new curriculum ideas or class projects).

Although schools often had an LEF and a booster club, PTA, or PTO operating at the same time, none of the schools we visited had a PTA, PTO, and booster club operating together. The schools that had a PTO or booster club instead of a

Table 4.3

School-Based and District-Based Entities Channeling Private Resources to Schools and Districts

School-Based	District-Based
Principal (10)	District staff (6)
LEF (7)	LEF (5)
PTA (6)	Superintendent (3)
School-site/leadership council (6)	Advisory board (1)
District staff (4)	Booster club (0)
Booster club (2)	Other school-based club/association (0)
Other school-based club/associations (1)	Principal (0)
PTO (1)	PTA (0)
Advisory board (0)	PTO (0)
Superintendent (0)	School-site/leadership council (0)

PTA typically said that they formed these organizations to avoid paying fees to the national PTA organization.

Whereas a number of schools had school-site/leadership councils, these groups generally did not directly raise private support. Instead, they often helped formulate priorities in terms of a school's need and provided guidance to parents or principals on how best to approach potential private sponsors. In addition, school-site/leadership councils often directed the allocation of private support, based on stated priorities, once funds reached the schools.

Four of the schools reported receiving help from district staff to attract private support. These schools reported that their districts informed them about available grants and provided the services of a grant writer. In addition, these districts referred potential private givers to their schools.

At the District Level

Each of the districts had district staff at some level responsible for private giving. Three of the districts had one or more full-time positions devoted to attracting and maintaining private support while the rest of the districts included these tasks as just another part of a staff member's job description. The district interviewees generally stated that district staff assumed a variety of roles in helping schools attract private support—for example, organizing special events, establishing school-business partnerships, or providing grant-writing assistance. However, the schools in general were *not* well informed about district activities. Although all of the districts said they had staff devoted to attracting private support and conducting various fund-raising activities that benefited the schools, only four of the ten schools in our sample cited any district role in their fund-raising efforts, suggesting a lack of communication between some districts and schools.

In our sample, the LEFs had closer connections with the districts than with the schools. Four of the six districts reported that a LEF played a role in attracting private support to their district. Because of their close connection with the LEFs,[3] these districts also reported a good understanding of the range of activities undertaken by the foundations. In addition, when district staff was asked about the types of private support the districts obtained, support from a LEF was often included in the discussion. In contrast, schools did not stress the importance of

---

[3]Information on the range of LEF activities was collected through phone interviews with LEFs, as documented in Appendix D.

LEFs and oftentimes school personnel did not have a good understanding of the LEF's involvement with schools or the district as a whole.

Only three districts in our sample responded that the superintendent played a role in raising private support. This is probably because we spoke directly with the superintendent at only two of the districts we visited. In the other districts, we relied on the staff telling us independently that the superintendent had a role in attracting private support. If we had prompted the staff about the role of the superintendent, or if we had spoken directly with the superintendents, this number would likely have been higher.

One school district had a formal partnership between it and local business leaders, community groups, city officials, and local school supporters. The partnership members took an active role and encouraged community members to become involved in their local schools by volunteering their time to "job-shadowing" programs and career days and by teaching mini-courses in art, music, or other disciplines. The partnership had an advisory committee that included the more-active members of the community and school district. Advisory committee members also acted as "ambassadors" to the community, promoting involvement in the various district programs.

Mechanisms to Attract Private Resources

Our interviews with school and district personnel revealed that individuals and organizations used a number of mechanisms to attract private support. Table 4.4 lists those mechanisms, which were employed by the schools and districts in our sample to attract both monetary and in-kind private support. The numbers in parentheses represent the number of schools or districts mentioning a specific mechanism used to raise private support.

At the School Level

Schools rely most heavily on personal contacts/relationship building, product sales, and special events to attract private resources. In fact, almost every school principal emphasized the importance of personal contacts and relationship building.

While all principals relied on contacts and relationship building to some extent, some principals spent more time and energy in this endeavor than others. One principal, for example, called parents to offer a personal thank-you for their

Table 4.4

Mechanisms to Attract Private Resources in School and District Sample

Schools	Districts
Personal contacts/relationship building (9)	Personal contacts/relationship building (6)
Product sales (9)	Grant applications (4)
Special events (7)	School-business partnerships (4)
Grant applications (4)	Special events (3)
Mail solicitation (4)	High-profile speakers/hosts (2)
School-business partnerships (4)	K–12 higher-education partnerships (1)
Participation in scrip or Web site programs (3)	Link with city planning (1)
	Local and national presentations (1)
Local newspaper advertising (1)	Mail solicitation (1)
Peer pressure (1)	Product sales (1)
Phone solicitation (1)	Professional fund-raiser (1)
Professional fund-raiser (1)	Local newspaper advertising (0)
K-12 higher-education partnerships (0)	Participation in scrip or Web site programs (0)
Local and national presentations (0)	
High-profile speakers/hosts (0)	Peer pressure (0)
Link with city planning (0)	Phone solicitation (0)

contributions. Another principal, who had been in the same school for almost 20 years, attributed her success in this area to her longevity in the position. She explained that longevity leads to stronger and more-extensive networks, which increase the likelihood of attracting resources.

Almost every principal also mentioned the importance of product sales, which ran the gamut from operating a student-run store to selling baked goods, candy, and wrapping paper. The schools also sponsored special events, such as auctions, raffles, swap meets, and carnivals, designed to attract private monetary support. In addition, schools often organized special events that garnered in-kind support, such as school beautification days, career days, and principal-for-a-day programs.

A smaller number of schools relied on mail solicitations, grant applications, and school-business partnerships. However, at those schools, these mechanisms were key components of their strategy to attract private resources. For example, one school sent out a letter at the beginning of the school year asking each parent for monetary support, and even suggesting a particular dollar amount.

Successful grant applications often helped schools to support after-school programs, fund the purchase of computers and other forms of technology, and, in one case, fund an additional administrative staff member. Whereas the forms of private giving just mentioned tended to consist of one-time donations, school-business partnerships often afforded schools a more-steady source of support. Typically, business partners offered a variety of in-kind support, such as student mentoring and tutoring, but partnerships that were maintained over time sometimes led to monetary support for the school as well. Interestingly, most of the principals we interviewed emphasized that in-kind support was *more* valuable to them than monetary support.

Some school principals mentioned additional mechanisms for generating support. In one affluent community, for example, the PTA distributed a letter to parents that reported on each family's level of giving. The PTA chose to do this after hearing some of the parents say they did not know that the school needed their support. The letter ended up serving two purposes—it helped to get the word out that the school needed support and it used an element of peer pressure to motivate parents to contribute.

At the District Level

The school districts in our sample used a variety of mechanisms to attract private support, which they in turn allocated to individual schools. As did the principals, superintendents and district-level staff also relied heavily on personal contacts and relationship building to attract private resources, although they tended to focus their efforts on different types of private givers than the schools did. Both the schools and districts made the effort to develop and nurture relationships with local businesses. Schools, however, also focused their efforts on parents, whereas districts were more likely to pursue relationships with corporations.

The next most-widely used strategies at the district level were grant applications and development of school-business partnerships. Grant writing, as a mechanism for obtaining private resources, appears to be more of a district-level activity than a school-level one, in large part because districts are more likely to have enough resources to support a staff grant writer. Several of our sample districts employed grant writers who pursue grants on behalf of their district and support school-level grant writing. One grant that a district was successful in pursuing was awarded through Hewlett-Packard's Telementors Program, which provides teachers with laptop computers and Internet access. Another district mentioned that the National Education Association had awarded grants to several individual teachers in the district.

The most common form of school-business partnerships followed the "adopt-a-school" model, through which a local business partners with a particular school to provide multiple forms of support. These partnerships ranged from very formalized programs with well-known businesses, often organized or coordinated by the district, to informal associations on a smaller scale, such as between a school and a local retailer. One school in our study was in its second year of a partnership with the Federal Bureau of Investigation, which involved agents visiting the school once a month to mentor students. One of the districts in our sample partnered with Intel Corporation to design and set up its computing network, while another received a substantial amount of money from a major gas utility company for educational resources related to math and science.

In contrast to the aforementioned partnerships with high-profile corporations, many of the schools in our sample had multiple informal relationships with local business owners. For example, a landscaping company provided help with "school beautification days" and a hardware store donated supplies for school repairs.

Districts also host special events, although they are less prevalent at the district level than the school level. For example, the districts frequently organize principal-for-a-day events, which have become quite popular. One district organized one such event that involved all schools in the district getting at least one guest from the business community to serve as school "principal." At the end of the event, the district gathered together the participants to discuss the experience and received very positive feedback. In addition, districts host special events to provide support to schools' efforts to attract private giving. For example, several districts hosted breakfast meetings to recognize local supporters of district schools. This helped the schools attract additional local support by showing the schools that the districts were behind them and by providing a means to publicly recognize the generosity of local businesses.

Although the districts actively raise support for the schools, principals consistently reported that the share of private resources that the schools themselves secure is greater than the share they receive from the districts. This may be due, in part, to districts allocating funds across a large number of schools. In addition, schools may receive relatively large in-kind contributions, particularly of the volunteer type.

Types of Private Giving

Tables 4.5, 4.6, and 4.7 list the types of in-kind volunteer time, in-kind material donations, and monetary giving, respectively, received by schools and districts in our sample. The numbers in parentheses in the tables represent the number of schools or districts that mentioned receiving a specific type of private giving.

Although it is difficult to quantify the dollar value of in-kind material and volunteer time donations, respondents were able to estimate the relative value of those contributions in comparison with monetary contributions.

Table 4.5

Types of In-Kind Private Giving in School and District Sample: Volunteer Time

Schools	Districts
Enrichment programs (5)	Family services (3)
Student tutoring (5)	After-school programs (2)
Classroom support (4)	Enrichment programs (2)
School facilities (4)	School/district promotion (2)
Administrative (2)	Staff training (1)
School/district promotion (2)	Student support services (1)
Student mentoring (2)	Student tutoring (1)
After-school programs (1)	Administrative (0)
Family services (1)	Classroom support (0)
Staff training (1)	School facilities (0)
Student support services (1)	Student instruction (0)
Student instruction (0)	Student mentoring (0)

Table 4.6

Types of In-Kind Private Giving in School and District Sample: Material Donations

Schools	Districts
Supplies/equipment (8)	Technology (5)
Instructional materials (6)	Supplies/equipment (3)
Technology (6)	Instructional materials (2)
Awards/gift certificates (5)	Off-site facilities for events (2)
Student/family supplies (4)	Student/family supplies (1)
Food (2)	Awards/gift certificates (0)
Off-site facilities for events (2)	Food (0)

Table 4.7

Types of Monetary Private Giving in School and District Sample

Schools	Districts
Donations (9)	Donations (6)
Percentage of product sales (6)	Leasing of facilities and services (1)
Membership dues (1)	Membership dues (0)
Wills/bequests (1)	Paid endorsements/advertising revenue (0)
Leasing of facilities and services (0)	Percentage of product sales (0)
Paid endorsements/advertising revenue (0)	Scholarships (0)
Scholarships (0)	User fees (0)
User fees (0)	Wills/bequests (0)

At the School Level

No one type of volunteer activity appears to dominate across the schools; different schools receive different kinds of volunteer support. One-half of the schools have student tutoring programs, often involving local businesspeople or community members who visit the schools for one-on-one reading sessions with students to improve the students' language skills.

One school attributed the success of its tutoring program to the fact that it provided training to volunteers from the business community. The volunteer tutors were asked to work with students who had fallen behind in their studies. When the school told the volunteers that they would receive training on how to help the students, it added to their interest in volunteering and their enthusiasm for the program.

One-half of the schools also received volunteer help to staff enrichment programs. For example, for one of the schools, a juvenile delinquency prevention center offered classes for parents and leadership programs for students. At another school, a local art museum offered an art education program.

Fewer than half the schools reported receiving classroom support. This is somewhat surprising given that one would expect most schools to have at least a few parents volunteering at some level in the classroom. Because classroom support is such an integral part of the operation of a school, it is possible that some principals did not think to mention this support as part of the private giving their schools received. Nevertheless, classroom support was mentioned relatively more often than most other types of volunteer-time options.

Two of the schools had student mentor programs in which students were paired with "buddies" from the community. These mentor-student pairs engaged in a variety of activities including exchanging letters or e-mail messages, spending lunch breaks together, and student visits to the mentor's workplace. These mentoring relationships often began with very small time commitments, such as monthly e-mail communications, and then blossomed over time into stronger connections between the mentor and student.

The majority of schools received material donations of instructional materials, computers and other technology items, supplies and equipment, and awards and gift certificates. Supplies and equipment ranged from copying machines to paper and books. Local businesses donated awards and gift certificates to recognize various achievements, including outstanding student attendance or student performance, or for teacher recognition. Four schools received miscellaneous supplies for students and their families, which most often consisted of school uniforms. Hotels donated meeting space to two schools, and two other schools received food from local businesses to serve at special events.

The vast majority of schools received some level of monetary donations from a variety of private givers. We discuss the relative size of these donations across schools later in this chapter. Interview respondents noted that corporate and business donors generally begin by providing in-kind support and then, as a relationship develops, some givers would eventually provide monetary support as well.

We found that monetary donations were almost always targeted for a specific purpose or program. Generally, schools first developed priorities, plans, or goals, and then approached private givers with specific proposals. Schools then engaged in a dialogue with potential donors in order to match those donors with proposals that would also meet their needs.

Private monetary support, therefore, was not totally flexible in that it was usually given to support a specific program or goal. This type of support was somewhat flexible, however, in that the purpose for the funding was typically outlined by the school and refined through discussions with the sponsor. For example, one school located next to a major freeway wanted to build a wall as a barrier against highway noise and pollution. The business community did not support the initial proposal for the wall. After conversations with members of the local community, the school decided instead to plant trees to help separate the freeway from the school. Sponsors purchased individual trees and received special recognition at a school ceremony, and their names were placed on a plaque next to the trees they donated.

Schools also received monetary support through a variety of percentage-of-sales programs. Some businesses offered programs whereby parents could apply for a credit card with a business and a percentage of their purchases on that card would be donated to a designated school. Schools also received a percentage of sales through scrip programs (see Chapter 2). A large cereal manufacturer sponsored a program that allowed parents to mail in cereal box tops and in return receive points, which were then converted into flexible "money" for their children's school. Schools reported that the total quantity of funds gained from these percentage-of-sales programs was generally very small, but nonetheless important in purchasing some extras for the schools. Money obtained through scrip or other percentage-of-sales programs was usually truly flexible in how it could be used.

School principals had a difficult time quantifying the levels of both in-kind and monetary support, particularly in-kind support. This is not surprising, what with the variety of private donors giving to various school programs. For example, parents provided a variety of in-kind support, such as donating supplies to their children's classrooms, volunteering in the school office, providing administrative help to teachers, and helping to plan and run fund-raising events.

One principal suggested that he could not reasonably be expected to be aware of every PTA, PTO, or booster club activity, or know exactly how much time parents in these organizations spend on product sales and special events. Similarly, it would be difficult for school staff to quantify the time that community members contribute to student enrichment or after-school programs. With that said, principals uniformly agreed that in-kind support well outweighs monetary support in terms of quantity. In addition, they generally put greater value on in-kind support (particularly volunteer support) than monetary support.

At the District Level

The districts in our sample typically obtained less volunteer time and fewer material donations than the schools, and concentrated more heavily on securing monetary donations. About one-half of the districts did, however, receive volunteer support for family services that were provided at the school level. Family services covered a number of areas. Several of the districts, for example, formed relationships with healthcare providers to establish health services on school campuses. Other districts received volunteer support to provide parenting classes or English language instruction to parents. In addition, about one-third of the districts secured volunteer support for enrichment and after-school programs. In a few districts, individuals volunteered by participating in district fund-raisers.

Districts generally focused more heavily than the schools on pursuing monetary donations from large givers in order to support their larger-scale, district-wide programs. For example, one district received a donation of several hundred thousand dollars from a large philanthropic foundation to provide professional development for teachers and develop programs to raise parental involvement in the schools. Another district received about $100,000 from a large corporation to help develop its high school and middle school math and science departments and programs.

Neither districts nor schools obtained paid endorsements or advertising revenue, and the majority of them explicitly stated that they oppose receiving such revenue. One district stated that an Internet access provider offered 15 computers for each junior high and high school in the district, each of which had around 300 students. The offer included an exclusivity clause barring the district from using another Internet provider for three years. The district refused the offer because of the exclusivity agreement. Another district will not allow donors to distribute promotional literature for students to take home with them without first obtaining district approval.

Usage of Private Monetary Giving

Private monetary giving supports a wide range of activities that typically fall into three main categories: current operations, technology, and capital improvements. As stated earlier, most monetary giving, except for the generally small amount of funds coming from percentage of sales, tends to be targeted to particular functions or goals. Table 4.8 lists the various uses of private monetary giving at our sample schools and districts. The numbers in parentheses represent the number of schools or districts mentioning a specific type of usage.

Table 4.8

Use of Private Monetary Giving in School and District Sample

Schools	Districts
Current Operations	**Current Operations**
Curricular enrichment programs (9)	Curricular enrichment programs (5)
School supplies/equipment (6)	Instructional materials (4)
Other staff salaries (5)	Professional development (3)
Instructional materials (3)	Athletics (2)
Professional development (3)	Health services (2)
Special events (2)	Special events (2)
Teacher aide positions (2)	Early childhood education (1)
Athletics (1)	Other staff salaries (1)
Health services (1)	Parent education programs (1)
Classroom teacher positions (0)	School supplies/equipment (1)
Early childhood education (0)	Student supplies (1)
Parent education programs (0)	Teacher aide positions (1)
Promotion of school/business partnerships (0)	Classroom teacher positions (0)
Salary enhancement or stipends for existing teachers (0)	Promotion of school/business partnerships (0)
School maintenance (0)	Salary enhancement or stipends for existing teachers (0)
Student supplies (0)	School maintenance (0)
Student transportation (0)	Student transportation (0)
Technology	**Technology**
Computers/software (2)	Computers/software (5)
Capital Improvements	**Capital Improvements**
Building enhancements (3)	Building enhancements (1)
School beautification (3)	Building additions (0)
Furniture (1)	Electrical wiring (0)
Building additions (0)	Furniture (0)
Electrical wiring (0)	Heating/air conditioning (0)
Heating/air conditioning (0)	Playground equipment (0)
Playground equipment (0)	School beautification (0)
Sports facilities (0)	Sports facilities (0)

At the School Level

Schools used private monetary support most often on curricular enrichment programs, such as field trips and after-school programs. The majority of schools also used private dollars for school supplies or equipment and salaries for other staff.[4] None of the schools or districts used private donations to purchase classroom teacher positions. Some school and district personnel stated that donations were too uncertain from year to year to commit to additional teaching positions based on the promise of those donations. Two schools that brought in considerable private support did, however, hire teacher aides for their classrooms.

Whereas only two schools stated that they purchased computers and other technology with private monies, a majority of school districts purchased technology with private support. One explanation for this difference is that decisions on technology tend to fall to a more-central planning body. In addition, technology purchases may require larger donations, which the districts receive more often than do the individual schools.

Somewhat surprising is the relatively small number of schools that used private monetary support for professional development. The studies of LEFs cited in Appendix D suggest that professional development is a common use of private dollars raised by LEFs. Possibly, we did not see professional support mentioned in our sample because the LEFs were not key players at most of the schools and districts that we visited.

Three schools used private monetary support for building enhancements and school beautification efforts. In terms of building enhancements, one school remodeled its auditorium and another school remodeled its library, and in terms of school beautification, one school purchased trees while another had the school building painted.

At the District Level

Districts most often used privately donated money to support curricular enrichment programs, purchase instructional material, and support professional development. Curricular enrichment programs included the implementation of science, reading, math and after-school programs and funding of academic

---

[4]"Other staff" includes consultants such as art or music teachers and reading and mathematics specialists.

decathlon teams. A majority of districts also used private monetary support to purchase computers and other technology.

A number of other programs, such as athletics, health services, and the financing of special events, were supported, to a lesser extent, through monetary contributions from the community. When deciding how to allocate funds or resources to schools, district staff generally stated that they distribute the money where the greatest need exists.

Differences in Private Giving at Schools and Districts by Socioeconomic Status

We observed some differences in the nature of private giving in schools and school districts given their varying socioeconomic status. The socioeconomic status of the families of school children may affect private giving for a variety of reasons. For example, parents in wealthier communities can make larger monetary donations to their children's schools. On the other hand, poorer communities may be able to solicit foundation or corporate giving that can be tied to the socioeconomic conditions in those communities. Further, middle- and lower-income communities might use a wide array of mechanisms to attract private giving, whereas wealthier communities might focus on a few large fund-raising events.

Effect of School Socioeconomic Status on Private Giving

Table 4.9 reveals patterns of private support according to the socioeconomic status of schools in our sample. In the table, schools are identified by letter only and listed from the lowest student participation in the federally funded Free and Reduced Price Lunch Program to the highest student participation in the program.[5] With participation ranging from 6 to 97 percent, School H had the smallest percentage of participation and School G had the highest.

Table 4.9 lists the private givers to each school in our sample, the entities that channel private resources to each school, the mechanisms the schools use to channel private resources, the types of private giving, and the usage of private monetary support. Some items in Table 4.9 are in boldface, indicating that the school experienced significant activity in that type of private giving.

---

[5]This is a proxy for affluence—lower participation is an indicator of greater affluence and higher participation is an indicator of lesser affluence.

Table 4.9

Patterns of Private Support in Schools According to Socioeconomic Status

School	Private Givers	Entity Channeling Private Resources	Mechanism to Attract Private Resources	Type of Private Giving	Use of Private Monetary Giving
H	Community members Corporations **Local businesses** **Parents** Professional associations	District Staff **LEF** **Principal** **PTA** School-site/leadership council	**Mail solicitation** **Peer pressure** **Personal contacts/ relationships** Product sales Professional fund-raiser Scrip or Web site programs Special events	IN-KIND Administrative Awards/gift certificates Classroom support Enrichment programs Off-site facilities for events School/district promotion Student tutoring Technology MONETARY **Donation** Membership Dues Percentage of Sales	Building enhancement Computers/software Curricular enrichment Instructional materials Other staff salaries Professional development School beautification School supplies/equipment Teacher aide positions
J	City government **Parents**	LEF Principal PTA School-site/leadership council	**Mail Solicitation** Personal contacts/relationships Phone solicitation Scrip or Web site programs Special events	IN-KIND Administrative Classroom support Instructional materials School supplies/equipment School/district promotion Technology MONETARY **Donation** Percentage of sales	Computers/software Curricular enrichment Furniture Instructional materials Other staff salaries Professional development School supplies/equipment Teacher aide positions

Table 4.9—Continued

School	Private Givers	Entity Channeling Private Resources	Mechanism to Attract Private Resources	Type of Private Giving	Use of Private Monetary Giving
C	**Community members** Local businesses **Parents**	LEF Other school-based associations Principal PTA School-site/leadership council	Personal contacts/ relationships Product sales School-business partnerships Scrip or Web site programs Special events	IN-KIND Classroom support Instructional materials School facilities School supplies/ equipment Technology MONETARY Donation Percentage of sales	Building enhancement Instructional materials Special events
I	Community-based organization Local businesses Parents Students	LEF Principal PTA School-site/leadership council	Personal contacts/ relationships Product sales Special events	IN-KIND Awards/gift certificates Enrichment programs Food Off-site facilities for events School facilities Student tutoring MONETARY Donation	Curricular enrichment Other staff salaries School supplies/ equipment

Table 4.9—Continued

School	Private Givers	Entity Channeling Private Resources	Mechanism to Attract Private Resources	Type of Private Giving	Use of Private Monetary Giving
B	Alumni **Community members** Community-based organization Corporations Local businesses Parents Philanthropic foundations Professional associations	District Staff LEF **Principal** PTA	Grant applications **Personal contacts/ relationships** Product sales School-business partnerships Special events	IN-KIND Awards/gift certificates Enrichment programs Instructional materials School facilities School supplies / equipment Student tutoring Student/family supplies MONETARY Donation	Athletics Building enhancement Curricular enrichment Other staff salaries School beautification
F	Advocacy group Community-based organization Corporations **Local businesses** Parents Students	**Booster club** District staff LEF Principal	Grant applications Mail solicitation **Personal contacts/ relationships** Product sales School business partnerships	IN-KIND Instructional materials School facilities School supplies / equipment Student mentoring Student tutoring Student/family supplies MONETARY Donation Percentage of sales	Curricular enrichment School beautification School supplies/ equipment

Table 4.9—Continued

School	Private Givers	Entity Channeling Private Resources	Mechanism to Attract Private Resources	Type of Private Giving	Use of Private Monetary Giving
A	City government Community-based organization Corporations Local businesses Parents Philanthropic foundations Students	Booster club **Principal**	Grant applications Local newspaper advertising **Personal contacts/ relationships** Product sales School-business partnerships Special events	IN-KIND Enrichment programs Instructional materials School supplies/equipment Student tutoring Student/family supplies Technology MONETARY Donation Wills/bequests	Curricular enrichment Other staff salaries
E	Other public agencies Parents Philanthropic foundations	District staff Principal PTA	Mail solicitation Personal contacts/ relationships Product sales	IN-KIND Awards/gift certificates School supplies/equipment Student mentoring Technology MONETARY Donation	Curricular enrichment School supplies/ equipment

Table 4.9—Continued

School	Private Givers	Entity Channeling Private Resources	Mechanism to Attract Private Resources	Type of Private Giving	Use of Private Monetary Giving
D	Community-based organization Corporations Local businesses Parents	Principal PTA School-site/leadership council	Product sales Special events	IN-KIND Food School supplies/equipment Technology MONETARY Percentage of sales	Curricular enrichment Special events
G	Advocacy group City government Colleges/universities **Community-based organizations** Corporations **Local businesses** Parents Professional associations	LEF Principal PTO School-site/leadership council	Grant applications Personal contacts/relationships Product sales	IN-KIND After-school programs Awards/gift certificates Classroom support Enrichment programs Family services Instructional materials School supplies/equipment Staff training Student support services Student/family supplies MONETARY Donation Percentage of sales	Curricular enrichment Health services Professional development School supplies/equipment

NOTES: Schools are listed from the lowest percentage of student participation in the federally funded Free and Reduced Lunch Program (School H) to the highest percentage of participation (School G). Boldface type indicates that the schools experienced significant activity in that type of private support.

We used a number of mechanisms to determine whether a school was particularly active in certain types of private giving—for example, when an interviewee explicitly mentioned an item as playing an especially active role at a school or district without any prompting from us. In many cases, the interviewee did not explicitly state that a type of private support was especially active at his or her school or district, but it was clear through the course of the interview that the type of private giving played a key role.[6]

For example, whereas all schools had parents who gave to their children's school, the degree of parental giving varied tremendously. At some schools, parental involvement was limited to a few parents spending a relatively small amount of time in organizing a school fund-raiser. At other schools, a great number of parents were actively involved in a variety of roles at the school—for example, volunteering in classrooms, contributing to fund-raisers, and participating in school planning. In some cases, the interviewee noted the degree to which parents were active in the school or district by using specific examples. In other cases, it was clear through the course of the interview the degree to which parents were active in the school or district. Finally, in other cases, it was either explicitly mentioned by the interviewee that parents were involved in the school or district but not to a significant degree, or it was obvious from the interview that parents were involved slightly or not at all.

As Table 4.9 shows, schools located in the highest-level socioeconomic communities had very strong parental support in absolute terms and very strong parental support relative to the other schools in the sample. At all schools, regardless of socioeconomic status, parents provided monetary as well as in-kind support, which included volunteering in classrooms and at school fund-raisers.

Whereas schools in wealthier communities had a greater overall level of parental support, some schools in poorer communities were successful in raising other types of private support, although they often needed to approach a wider array of private donors than did most of the wealthier schools. To some degree, the list of private givers to schools was longer at schools in poorer communities because the schools could not rely as readily on parent support. In addition, schools in poorer communities had some options for private giving that were not available in more-affluent communities. Several interview respondents suggested that some donors focus their efforts on less-advantaged communities where they feel the need for help is greatest. This seemed to be particularly true of philanthropic foundations, corporations, and community-based organizations.

---

[6]For an item to be viewed as being especially active, the RAND research team, through a consensus, designated the item as such.

Although the wealthier schools in our sample relied on relatively few private givers, those schools generally used a relatively large number of mechanisms to attract private support from those givers. The two wealthiest schools in our sample used mail and/or phone solicitations to request monetary donations from parents, whereas the rest of the schools did not. In addition, it is the wealthier communities that participate in the scrip or Web site programs for raising private monetary support. It is not clear why schools in our sample in the middle and lower end of the socioeconomic scale do not participate in these programs. The poorer schools in our sample did not have strong parent associations and perhaps such organizations are key to operating scrip and Web site programs. Some principals in the poorer communities stated that because these programs are dependent on parents spending dollars on purchases that result in money back to the schools, the programs did not provide enough funds to warrant their schools becoming involved in them.

Personal contacts and relationship building appear to be particularly important mechanisms to attract private support at schools in the middle and lower end of the socioeconomic scale. These schools could not rely as readily on parental monetary and in-kind support as did schools in the wealthier communities. Instead, to attract private support, less-affluent schools were dependent on a dynamic school principal who was interested in making connections in the community in order to attract and maintain support.

The wealthier schools had a strong focus on securing direct monetary donations, particularly from parents. At the same time, even the wealthiest schools in our sample stated that private monetary contributions accounted for less than 5 percent of their total operating budget. Wealthier schools also received sizable in-kind contributions from parents volunteering their time at the schools. Schools located in communities at the middle and lower end of the socioeconomic scale appeared to have at least as much in-kind private support as the wealthier communities, but the support came from a different sort of private giver, such as a local business or community-based organizations.

It is difficult to get a sense of the relative size of the in-kind contributions because volunteer time is difficult to measure. But the *variety* of private givers who contributed their time to the schools was greater at schools in the middle and lower socioeconomic brackets.

The relatively large size of monetary donations made to the two schools located in the wealthiest communities was apparent given the number and type of items those schools purchased with the donations. School H and School J had a relatively long list of items that they purchased with private monetary giving. In addition, both schools used their private monetary donations to fund part-time teacher aide positions (non-salary positions with no benefits) for a significant number of their classrooms.

Schools at all wealth levels consistently used private monetary giving for curriculum enrichment programs. Those programs included an arts curriculum, an environmental garden project, a full-inclusion program for deaf students, and a variety of field trips. Monetary contributions were also used for "other staff" salaries by schools in all socioeconomic brackets.[7]

Effect of District Socioeconomic Status on Private Giving

Table 4.10 documents patterns of private giving to each school district in our sample. Districts are listed from lowest (District E) to highest (District C) according to the percentage of students participating in the Free and Reduced Price Lunch Program. Six to 97 percent of the student population in each school in the districts in our sample participated in the program. As in Table 4.9, items shown in boldface indicate the types of private support in which the school districts were particularly active. [8]

Local businesses and corporations are significant private givers who give on a regular basis. This is true across school districts, regardless of the relative wealth of the district. As Table 4.10 indicates, local businesses were frequently mentioned as playing a significant role in private giving in the more-affluent districts, whereas corporations were mentioned as being particularly active in providing support to the district with the lowest socioeconomic status. Some of the staff members in that district stated that corporations frequently preferred to focus their efforts where they perceive the greatest need to be, which tends to be in lower-income communities. For example, in District C, a large corporation

---

[7]The "other staff" included a science consultant, noontime supervisors, school nurses, and a reading specialist.

[8]We also examined the effect of district size on private giving. The wealth and size of the districts in our sample are highly correlated and therefore may hide patterns specifically related to either the size or socioeconomic status of a district. For example, the three smallest districts in our sample are also the three wealthiest. With that said, a few patterns appear that are based on the size of a district which are worth noting. The largest district in the sample was an active player in attracting and receiving private support. The size of the district allowed for several full-time positions devoted to various aspects of securing private giving. In addition, the size of a district helped it to attract high-profile speakers, who in turn attracted media attention to the district. Larger districts were also particularly active in attracting support from local businesses. The smallest (and wealthiest) school districts had a wider range of uses for their private monetary gifts than the bigger districts, which concentrated on a few large-scale programs.

Table 4.10

Patterns of Private Support in Districts According to Socioeconomic Status

District	Private Givers	Entity Channeling Private Resources	Mechanism to Attract Private Resources	Type of Private Giving	Use of Private Monetary Giving
E	Colleges/universities Community members Community-based organizations Corporations **Local businesses** Other public agencies Parents **Philanthropic foundations**	**District staff** LEF	**Grant applications** **Personal contacts/ relationships** Product sales **Special events**	IN-KIND After-school programs School/district promotion Technology MONETARY **Donation**	Athletics Building enhancement Computers/software Curricular enrichment Health services Instructional materials Other staff salaries School supplies/equipment Special events
F	**City government** Community members Corporations Local businesses Parents Philanthropic foundations	District staff LEF Superintendent	**High-profile speakers/hosts** Personal contacts/ relationships Professional fund-raiser	IN-KIND Off-site facilities for events Supplies/equipment Technology MONETARY **Donation**	Computers/software Curricular enrichment Early childhood education Health services Instructional materials Professional development Teacher aide positions

Table 4.10—Continued

District	Private Givers	Entity Channeling Private Resources	Mechanism to Attract Private Resources	Type of Private Giving	Use of Private Monetary Giving
B	City government Colleges/universities Community-based organizations Corporations **Local businesses** Parents	**Advisory board** District staff LEF	Grant applications Personal contacts/ relationships **School-business partnerships**	IN-KIND Enrichment programs Instructional materials Supplies/equipment Technology MONETARY Donation	Athletics Curricular enrichment Instructional materials
D	City government Colleges/universi-ties Community members Community-based organiza-tions Corporations **Local businesses** Philanthropic foundations Professional association	**District staff** LEF Superintendent	Grant applications **High-profile speakers/hosts** K-12 –higher-education partnerships **Link with city planning** Local and national presentations **Personal contacts/relationship** School-business partnerships **Special events**	IN-KIND Family Services Instruc-sional materials School/district promotion Staff training Student support services Student/family supplies MONETARY Donation Leasing of facilities and services	Computers/software Curricular enrichment Instructional materials Parent education programs Professional development Special events

Table 4.10—Continued

District	Private Givers	Entity Channeling Private Resources	Mechanism to Attract Private Resources	Type of Private Giving	Use of Private Monetary Giving
A	Colleges/universities Community members Community-based organization Corporations Local businesses Parents	District staff LEF Superintendent	Grant applications Personal contacts/relationships School-business partnerships	IN-KIND Family services Off-site facilities for events Supplies/equipment Technology MONETARY Donation	Computers/software Student supplies
C	**Corporations** Local businesses	District staff	Mail solicitation Personal contacts/relationships School-business partnerships Special events	IN-KIND After-school programs Enrichment programs Family services Student tutoring Technology MONETARY Donation	Computers/software Curricular enrichment Professional development

NOTES: Districts are listed from the lowest percentage of student participation in the Free and Reduced Price Lunch Program (District E) to the highest percentage of participation (District C). Boldface type indicates that the districts experienced significant activity in that type of private support.

provides after-school math and science enrichment classes for the local schools and another large corporation runs parental training programs, with about 1,000 parents graduating from the program each year.

Consistent with the literature, LEFs were found across all districts in our sample; however, the two highest-income districts had particularly active LEFs. The LEF representative we interviewed in a less-wealthy community focused on a specific and relatively small contribution to the schools—providing school uniforms to low-income students. In contrast, the LEF in District E, the highest-income district, was able to provide arts and music programs, computers, and science labs to the local schools.[9]

Regardless of the income levels of families in the district, school districts rely on a variety of mechanisms to attract private support. Most districts were particularly active in at least one mechanism to attract private support, but this was not the case with the two lowest-income districts in our sample. Those two districts had specific leadership issues that likely prevented them from attracting private support. In particular, District A is located in a city where local government politics negatively affected the district's relationship with the surrounding community. District D, on the other hand, relied on a wide variety of mechanisms to attract private support. This appears to be a result of two related factors specific to District D: (1) It is a large district and can therefore dedicate several staff members to the task of attracting and coordinating private giving to the district, and (2) the district superintendent considers private support one of his priorities.

Similar to the situation at the school level, the higher-income districts relied most heavily on monetary donations, whereas the lower- and middle-income districts received a relatively large number of in-kind donations. The monetary contributions in the higher-income districts were larger in part because of the local education foundations. We do not know the relative size of the in-kind donations, but the middle- and lower-income districts received a greater variety of in-kind contributions and emphasized this type of support in our interviews with them. In addition, in-kind support in these districts resulted in programs of significant importance offering student support services and family services.

The differences in the monetary contributions across school districts are apparent when one examines the various uses of private monetary support. The two

---

[9]The LEF in District E has a close relationship with the school district. LEF staffers are located at the district office. As a result, the district personnel we interviewed considered funds raised by the LEF to be funds raised by the district office. This was not necessarily the case in the other districts in which the LEFs and the district staff acted more autonomously. The use of private monetary giving in District E includes the use of private monetary support raised by the LEF.

highest-income districts were able to support a wider array of activities with the monetary contributions they received. The wealthier the district, the more programs, services, and materials the district purchased with private monetary contributions. Similar to the situation at the school level, districts across socioeconomic levels earmarked monetary contributions to curriculum enrichment programs. Those programs included health and nutrition classes, physical education programs, teacher forums, and family literacy programs.

The observations presented in this chapter on schools and school districts of differing socioeconomic status are not meant to provide definitive conclusions, but rather building blocks for the development of hypotheses for future research. We hope that some of the observations in this pilot study can be used as testable hypotheses at the outset of future research that employs a larger sample of schools and districts and a survey instrument designed for testing these hypotheses.

Summary

This chapter offered insights into the *who, how,* and *what* of private involvement in public education by examining a sample of districts and schools in Los Angeles County. We also discussed how the socioeconomic status of families, as measured by student participation in the federally funded Free and Reduced Price Lunch Program affected patterns of private support in our sample districts and schools.

We found a vast array of givers to districts and schools, mechanisms to attract support, types of private giving, and uses of monetary support. We also found that socioeconomic status does appear to affect the patterns of giving, the means of attracting support, types of giving, and the use of gifts across districts and schools. Our key findings are as follows:

- Whereas parental involvement was the most common form of "giving" at the school level, other types of contributors also play a significant role in providing support to the schools. In particular, local businesses and corporations play key roles in supporting schools in their communities. However, little interaction exists between colleges or universities and the public schools.

- At every school in the sample, the principal was involved to at least to some degree in attracting private resources to their school. In general, principals took the lead in developing relationships and maintaining communications efforts with the community at large and other private sponsors. The role of the principal in securing private support was particularly significant in communities on the low end of the socioeconomic scale.

- School principals had a difficult time quantifying the exact value of both in-kind and monetary support, particularly in-kind support. With that said, principals uniformly agreed that in-kind support well outweighs monetary support in terms of the amount of support received. In addition, they generally put greater value on in-kind support (especially volunteer support) than monetary support.

- Monetary donations were almost always targeted for a specific purpose or program.

- Private giving was generally intended by the givers to be short-term, at least initially. This situation affected how schools decided to use private monetary support. Short-term support was most often used for curricular enrichment programs, such as field trips and after-school programs. Longer-term support could lead to changes in the actual curriculum, hiring of additional teacher aides, and other such benefits.

- Principals, superintendents, and district-level staff consistently emphasized the importance of personal contacts and relationship building in attracting private resources.

- Some differences existed between schools and districts in attracting private support. In general, school districts tended to attract resources from larger and more-organized groups, such as corporations, local businesses, and colleges and universities, as opposed to the schools' reliance on resources from smaller groups and associations and individuals.

- Most schools in our sample had very little interaction with the district LEF. Only one school regarded the LEF as a significant player in attracting private support. The LEFs appeared to have closer connections with the districts than with the schools. Even at the district level, the LEFs were seen as just one of many elements contributing to securing private support.

- The schools were generally not well informed about district efforts to attract private support, and were not well informed about district programs and staff that were available to support schools with their own efforts.

- Principals consistently reported that the share of private resources that the schools themselves raised was greater than the share of resources they received from the districts.

- Wealthier schools and school districts had a clear advantage in raising monetary contributions, particularly from parents, and tended to have more volunteer support from parents. Nevertheless, some schools in lower-income communities also had substantial private support, although it was of a different type and came from different sources. Lower-income communities were not necessarily at a disadvantage with respect to the *quantity* of private support, but they had to engage in more-extensive efforts to attract the support by casting a broad net across a variety of potential sources.

- Schools consistently stated that private monetary contributions accounted for less than 5 percent of their total operating budgets.

5. Lessons Learned from This Study

With the support of the John Randolph and Dora Haynes Foundation, we set out to examine, through our pilot study and this report, private support to public education. Although our sample of schools and districts was too small to make definitive conclusions, we nevertheless developed a number of recommendations that could be explored as hypotheses for future research, and as suggestions to consider for future policymaking.

The recommendations that follow offer both broad strategies for raising private support for public education and more-focused strategies to address the specific challenges of securing that support. Later in this chapter, we outline ways in which future research could be approached to expand the existing knowledge of private support to public education.

Broad-Based Strategies for Obtaining Private Support

The recommendations that follow offer some general strategies that may prove useful to schools and districts.

Maintain Continual Communication

One comment we heard repeatedly related to the importance of maintaining continual communication with the community at large. Principals, district super-intendents, and other interviewees noted the need for ongoing communication with parents, local businesses, corporate business partners, interested citizens, and other potential givers. This can be accomplished through various modes of communication including phone calls, newsletters, and face-to-face conversa-tions, which can be used to inform the community of any special events, the par-ticular needs of the schools, or even to just to send a thank-you for involvement with district or school activities. As one principal observed, you need to think about every person you meet every day because that person may some day bring needed resources to a school.

Make It a Reciprocal Relationship

Both school and district officials noted the importance of creating a reciprocal relationship with business partners so that both parties feel they are benefiting from the relationship. Business partners need a compelling reason to become involved with helping out schools. Principals, superintendents, and other school staff cited a number of reasons for the importance of outside involvement: an improved future labor force, increased publicity for the giver, better schools for the children of employees of local businesses, and the intrinsic benefits that derive from developing relationships that can help children in their schooling.

In addition, successful schools and districts made sure that members of the community knew they were valued and respected. The private givers were made to feel like partners, rather than just spectators, in the success of a school or district. To foster this relationship, community members were invited to participate in the planning of school projects and invited to schools for various events. Private givers were also recognized for their involvement. Something as simple as a personal thank-you letter from the principal or students went a long way in sustaining donor relations. In addition, several schools and districts had donor recognition events to honor those who supplied resources to the schools.

Finds Ways for Donors to "Get Their Feet Wet"

Several school principals noted that finding ways for community members to make modest contributions to support a school, and thereby gradually introduce donors to a school and its needs, is an especially effective strategy. After volunteers got a firsthand look at the schools and met the students, they frequently came back with more support.

For example, one school established a "buddy" program whereby students initially corresponded with community members by mail on a monthly basis. The community members were then invited to the school for "buddy breakfasts." After the sponsors got to know the students better and were made aware of the school's particular needs, they often became more involved in the school through reading programs and other volunteer efforts. Principal-for-a-day programs, award ceremonies to recognize students or volunteers, and other such activities can expose a school to the local community in small ways and help foster future relationships.

Make It Appealing for Individuals and Organizations to Become Involved

Districts and schools reported that they needed to be flexible and creative in their approach to making involvement appealing to prospective donors. Most successful schools and districts presented numerous ideas to businesses, parents, and other community members about how these potential donors could get involved in helping the schools, while remaining open to alternative ideas and suggestions.

The process of getting people involved with the schools often required ongoing conversations and negotiations, and districts and schools needed to be receptive to community input. For example, one school wanted to build a concrete wall between the school building and an adjacent noisy freeway. The idea for the wall was not well received by possible supporters, so school officials used an alternative tactic. They suggested a more aesthetically appealing barrier of trees and were then able to get the support they needed. Community members not only found planting trees a more appealing option, they could make donations to purchase the trees in individuals' names.

Along the same lines, several school principals stated that successful schools make everyone feel welcome. Principals specifically mentioned that PTAs should not be seen as exclusive clubs. In addition, the scheduled times and formats of school events and club meetings should take into consideration those community members with scheduling and time constraints.

Provide Training to Volunteers

Providing orientation and/or training to community members who were interested in volunteering was another effective strategy used by some schools. For example, one school offered a tutoring program that enabled volunteers from the community to come into the school to help students with their reading. Many of those students had fallen behind in their studies and were therefore perceived to be more difficult to teach. The key to the school's success with the program was that the school told prospective volunteers up front that they would be trained to help the students, which added to the volunteers' enthusiasm and willingness to participate, and to their effectiveness as tutors.

Know Your Resource Base

School and district personnel discussed how the various characteristics of their communities affected how they approached the task of fund-raising. They suggested that identifying their resource base required an understanding of the local community and what it had to offer in terms of support. For instance, whereas wealthier districts and schools may be able to target parents to a greater degree, other districts and schools may need to be more creative in their approach and cast a wider net across a variety of potential sources.

We found that although districts and schools in low-income areas could not always generate a great deal of monetary support from parents, because of their perceived need they generally were more likely to receive grants and support from corporations or philanthropic organizations. In other cases, some districts had a strong local business community with a vested interest in becoming involved with the local schools, whereas other districts without a strong local business community had to seek other avenues for support.

Small- to medium-size businesses tended to be more localized in their outreach efforts, limiting their giving to schools within their own communities. Large corporations are less geographically limited because they can afford to have a wider scope and because their customers and employees are more widely dispersed. Therefore, large corporations are more willing to assist schools outside of their geographic area.

In addition, the districts targeted a somewhat different set of givers and used different mechanisms for raising private support than did the schools. Corporations and LEFs tended to be more involved at the district level, whereas schools had greater interaction with individual parents, parent groups, and local businesses. Furthermore, districts generally received relatively large monetary contributions whereas schools were more effective in recruiting volunteer in-kind support.

In short, district and school officials should evaluate their resource base and create a fund-raising strategy that takes into account the most likely sources of funding.

Private Support Garners More Private Support

Staff members from several districts and schools noted that when a school or district can establish some credibility with potential givers, other givers (including foundations, corporations, and the like) are more willing to give. By securing private resources, a district or school established a precedent for asking others to donate. If a district or school exhibits a commitment to pursuing private support by receiving grants, developing local business partners, or building relationships with parents, other givers may also be interested in giving. Such support suggests that a school or district has educational programs worthy of private support, and the private contributions will be well used.

The Challenges of Raising Private Support and Suggested Strategies

The schools and districts in our sample faced some particularly difficult challenges in developing and maintaining private support. This section discusses some of those challenges and gives specific examples of what some schools and districts did to overcome them.

Time Demands

At every school in our sample, most of the responsibility for raising private support rested with the principal. However, most principals had difficulty finding the necessary time to develop game plans for obtaining private support and building relationships within the community. One principal addressed this problem by seeking a grant to fund the salary of a community liaison who could assume some of these tasks. Although the principal still initiated most of the external relationships and oversaw all the fund-raising activities, the community liaison handled much of the day-to-day communications and helped sustain the fund-raising efforts over time.

Turnover and Mobility

One of the challenges districts and schools consistently faced was turnover of key district or school staff and turnover of key contacts at businesses. Most of our interviewees had relatively short tenures at their current positions; several of the principals had been at their schools for only two or three years. Many interviewees suggested that longevity is a tremendous advantage in developing and maintaining relationships with parents, local businesses, corporations, and the community at large, and interviewees who had been in their positions for a relatively short period of time felt like they were at a disadvantage.

Building a new relationship with a donor, or stepping into a existing relationship established by a predecessor, usually takes a tremendous amount of effort. It was not clear how long or to what extent programs continued after a principal or superintendent left a school. One way to address the issue of turnover is to have more than one person at a school or district involved in building relationships with members of the local community.

In addition, foundations and corporations also experience personnel turnover, which can make it difficult for schools to build relationships with these organizations. A principal or superintendent's contact at a corporation is typically one specific individual. So, if that person changes jobs, the connection with the corporation can disappear, sometimes without notice. To address this problem, one staff member at a district with numerous business partnerships suggested that written contracts be used to formalize the relationship. It was also suggested that if a number of people from a business are involved in the partnership, the more likely it is the relationship would survive any one person's departure.

Short-term Support Mentality

In almost every case, district and school staff members noted that donors regarded donations and in-kind gifts as short-term commitments and not part of an ongoing program of giving. Although this short-term support can be viewed as an asset, and can lead to longer-term support, it can also require a large investment of staff time without an equivalent payoff. By developing an informal verbal "contract" with donors that specifies the level and type of giving, a longer-term commitment may result.

Not Knowing How to Attract Private Support

A number of school principals reported that they lacked knowledge on how to attract private support, and weren't sure how to go about getting that knowledge. Two principals in particular avoided developing relationships with potential donors from local businesses and the community at large because they did not feel comfortable in that role. Others reported that they learned how to approach potential donors through "trial and error," which may ultimately lead to frustration and negative experiences for both the donor and the recipient.

Several districts addressed this problem by making their staff grant writer available to assist schools in the district with identifying and applying for grants. Developing a working relationship with education foundations is another possible way to address this challenge. Foundation staff could handle fund-raising efforts so that principals and district staff can focus their attention on other matters.

Lack of Communication Between Districts and Schools

Poor communication between districts and schools can limit a school's ability to use available district support for attracting private resources. Schools seemed to have limited knowledge of services and programs the districts provided to help schools raise private support. In several cases, district staff told us about their various support-related activities, such as principal-for-a-day and adopt-a-school programs, or about staff members who were devoted to helping to attract private support, but the schools seemed to have little or no knowledge of them.

The communication problem was successfully addressed by one district that hosts monthly meetings with all the school principals in the district. The LEF director also attends the meetings, as do the PTA presidents. In this way, everyone stays informed about school- and district-level fund-raising efforts.

"Donor Fatigue"

District staff and school principals complained that a lot of competition can go on between schools and fund-raising organizations, resulting in a single business being asked for help by multiple groups. In addition, schools tended to operate independently in raising support for themselves, which meant that they were often unaware of what other schools were doing to attract private support. Adding to this, communication between schools and districts, which would have helped avoid overlap in approaching potential givers, was often lacking .

To address this problem, one district scheduled a monthly principals meeting, which not only facilitated internal communications but also helped ensure that multiple parties within the district were not approaching the same donors simultaneously. In addition, one of the main priorities of most LEFs is to develop a system-level approach to fund-raising. This includes coordinating their solicitation efforts with the district to avoid overlap, and having staff dedicated to tracking donors' past contributions and encouraging their future contributions.

Fear of Commercialization

Many district and school staff members noted their concern about the possibility of businesses being inappropriately involved with the schools. For this reason, most districts and schools avoided exclusivity contracts with business enterprises. Coca-Cola Company, for one, is backing away from exclusivity contracts in its vending machine operations in schools, and other corporations may follow Coca-Cola's lead.

Summary

For this study, we examined the existing literature, and interviewed principals, superintendents, district personnel, and LEF representatives to gain a better understanding of private support in public education. The issue of private resources in public education was virtually unexamined until our study. No systematic national data existed on the extent of private giving and how it varies across schools, nor did data exist on the strategies that encourage giving or how the resources from private funding are used.

What little research had been conducted in this area focused primarily on monetary donations and on local education foundations. As our pilot study has suggested, there is in fact a very wide array of types of giving, both monetary and in-kind, which provide additional resources for public schools. Through our analysis, we are able to provide a description of the flow of giving from donors to the end use by the schools and districts.

Policymakers, researchers, and the general public have voiced concerns over the possible inequities created by private contributions to public education. Decades of judicial and legislative action designed to equalize public spending across districts (and to a lesser extent schools) could be circumvented with the use of private resources. In other words, wealthier communities prohibited from raising additional public dollars could instead turn to other sources of support. Unfortunately, no data exist to determine if such a trend has indeed occurred. However, our preliminary research does not suggest that resource inequities, when taking into account both in-kind and monetary support, necessarily result from private support.

Whereas parental support is clearly greater at schools in higher-income areas, our research also suggests that schools in lower-income areas may have opportunities for raising additional resources that are not available to wealthier schools. For example, schools in poorer areas may have access to foundations or corporations that are striving to target their funding efforts to needy communities. Having said this, it is undoubtedly more difficult overall to generate additional support in low-income areas.

The disparity in parental involvement is a particularly difficult issue for policymakers to address because discouraging parental involvement at schools in high-income areas would be counterproductive. However, it is often difficult to increase parental involvement in schools in poorer communities because of the constraints facing many low-income parents. Clearly, a dedicated and energetic principal is an essential element in garnering parental and community involvement at schools in low-income areas. Therefore, anything that state and district officials can do to increase the placement of talented administrators in these schools is likely to lead to increased community involvement and a greater ability to secure private resources.

Policymakers and educators may want to explore other possible ideas to encourage private giving. For instance, state governments, counties, or districts could examine the possibility of providing training in effective strategies for raising private support. This could entail convening principals, superintendents, and other school and district personnel for formal training sessions to be lead by consultants or other experts. These conferences could also serve to promote information sharing. For instance, school and district representatives could share strategies that have, and have not, proved effective. Undoubtedly, some information sharing already takes place informally, but requiring principals and other educators to focus on innovative and successful strategies—and learn about failed ones—may minimize the likelihood of wasting precious time and effort on ventures that do not have a high probability of success.

We've presented just a few examples of the many possible initiatives that could be considered. Obviously, with further thought and deliberation, state and local policymakers may be able to develop a set of policies specifically designed to encourage private support for public schools.

Future Research

The analysis presented in this report represents a large step forward in our knowledge of the relationship between local communities and public schools. Nevertheless, we can continue to build on this knowledge with future research.

First and foremost, future research should include a larger sample of schools, which would provide a more-representative collection and allow for statistical analysis of differences across schools and communities. A larger sample would also allow for an examination across a number of geographic areas beyond Los Angeles County. Patterns of giving and uses of gifts may vary across different geographic areas, and examining those patterns may produce greater insights into the range of relationships between communities and public schools.

Second, future research should include the development of a survey that specifically probes districts and principals for answers to questions about monetary contributions, volunteer time, and in-kind gifts given to districts and schools. Although school officials may not know *exactly* how much is given to a district or school, a survey that includes at least a range of dollar values for monetary contributions would serve to improve the existing data. In addition, the survey should probe for various types of volunteer activities, the range of hours spent by volunteers in those activities, and an overall assessment of the quality of those hours. Questions in regard to the volunteer hours could be organized such that respondents would provide a range of the number of hours given to specific activities, and possibly assess the hourly value of the volunteer time.[1] A survey should also specifically ask school officials to provide an estimated value, or a range of the value, of in-kind gifts.

With the informational framework that a survey would provide, future researchers could more specifically assess the quantities and distribution of giving and determine how much value schools and districts place on different types of giving. This framework could also lead to greater insights into the degree to which districts and schools are circumventing equalized funding systems through private contributions. These sorts of analyses would be especially useful with a larger sample, where statistical analyses could be more meaningful and broader conclusions could be drawn.

Third, future research might include donor interviews and/or surveys, which could provide a greater understanding of why people and organizations give, and why businesses and organizations choose certain schools to support. Surveying donors may also serve to verify the estimated value of contributions to schools.

Fourth, future research could have a greater emphasis on business partnerships, which would provide additional insights into how these relationships are started in the first place and how they mature over time.

Our analysis summarizes the major themes of private support of public schools in Los Angeles County. Future studies could build upon this research to provide further answers to questions concerning why people and organizations give, how much they give, and whether statistical differences exist across various types of schools and communities.

---

[1]Respondents could be asked to state the hourly wage they would be willing to pay for the volunteer time, if they had the financial resources.

A. School Principal Interview Protocol

This appendix presents the protocol we used to obtain school principals' perspectives on private giving at their schools. The information we obtained from them was used in our analysis described in Chapter 4, and ultimately led to our conclusions presented in Chapter 5.

I. School Private Support

1. How has the role of private support—in-kind and monetary—changed over time in this school, if at all? What is the impetus for the changes?

2. What is the most important factor for a school to raise private support (for example, school personnel, active parents, thriving business community, or other factors)?

3. What is your role in attracting private support? How do you attract private resources to your school?

4. What organizations, if any, operate at your school to attract private support? (Interviewer probed for the following: PTA, PTO, booster club, LEF, school council, or other organization.)

5. What are the roles of the various organizations? How do the various organizations interact with each other? To what extent do the various organizations complement or compete with each other?

6. What mechanisms do the different organizations use to attract private resources? (Interviewer probed for the following: school fund-raisers, grants, mailings, personal contacts, phone solicitation, professional fund-raiser, other mechanisms). How do the mechanisms differ for different organizations?

7. If your district has a foundation, how does the school interact with the foundation?

8. Are there specific individuals within or outside of these organizations who are particularly involved in attracting private support to your school (for example, a particular parent or teacher)? Can we contact them?

9. Who are the private givers to your school? (Interviewer probed for the following: parents, philanthropic foundations, local businesses, religious organizations, colleges, corporations, other givers). How long has each of the givers been involved with your school?

10. How would you describe the local business environment? Are there local companies that are particularly active givers? Do local businesses tend to support a single school or more than one school in a neighborhood?

11. What types of private support does your school receive?

- What types of in-kind support? (Interviewer probed for the following: volunteer time, material donations, technical assistance, other types of support.)
- What types of monetary support? (Interviewer probed for the following: donations, percentage of sales, paid endorsements, user fees, leasing of facilities and services, other types of support.)

12. What is the quantity (or relative ranking) of the different types of in-kind and monetary private support?

13. What share of the school's budget is attributed to private monetary support? Attributed to in-kind support?

14. Does private giving tend to be discretionary or targeted? If discretionary, what percentage of the school's *flexible* budget is attributed to private monetary support?

15. Do private revenues tend to be more or less restricted in their use than public resources? What types of restrictions exist on the use of private resources (legal, targeted, any other)?

16. To what extent are private resources given for short-term versus long-term uses? Has the emphasis changed over time? Are programs generally re-funded?

17. Once private resources reach your school, how are decisions made about how they are allocated?

18. At what levels are they allocated (for example, school-wide improvements, or classroom, teacher, and/or student level)?

19. For what purposes are the private resources used? (Interviewer probed for the following: professional development, salaries, materials and supplies, curriculum enhancement programs, athletics, school maintenance, scholarships, other purposes.)

20. To what extent are private resources used to fund a lot of small projects at the school versus a few large projects? Has the emphasis changed over time?

21. What are the legal facilitators or hindrances to the collection and use of private support?

22. What are the downsides to collecting private resources? What kinds of equity issues, if any, are raised by the collection of private support? Are there circumstances under which you have, or would have to, refuse a contribution?

23. To what extent do private resources provide leverage for additional public and private support? To what extent do private resources crowd out public support?

24. For schools that receive categorical support, such as Title 1 funds, interviewers asked whether the collection of categorical aid influences efforts to collect private resources.

II. District Role

25. What support, if any, does your district provide to your school in its efforts to raise private support?

26. What is the relative quantity of private resources you receive from district efforts versus school efforts to obtain private support?

27. Do you act independently or do you work with other schools in your efforts to raise private support?

B. District Interview Protocol

This appendix presents the protocol we used to gain a district perspective on private giving at schools within each district. The information we obtained from district staff members was used in our analysis described in Chapter 4, and ultimately led to our conclusions presented in Chapter 5.

I. Private Support in District

1. How does your district attract private resources? What are the different fund-raising organizations?

2. Does your district have a designated person responsible for private giving?

3. Has your district used a professional fund-raising organization to raise private support? If so, what is the name of the organization?

4. If your district has a foundation, how does the district interact with the foundation?

5. Who are the private givers to the district (for example, parents, philanthropic foundations, local businesses, religious organizations, colleges, corporations, other givers)?

6. How would you describe the local business environment? Are there local companies that are particularly active givers?

7. What types of private support does your district receive?

- In-kind (volunteer time, material donations, school-to-work, other types of support)
- Monetary (donations, percentage of sales, paid endorsements, user fees, leasing of facilities and services, other types of support)

8. What is the quantity (or relative ranking) of the different types of in-kind and monetary private support?

9. What share of the district budget is attributed to private monetary support? Attributed to in-kind support?

10. What percentage of the district's *flexible* budget is attributed to private monetary support?

11. How are private resources (donations, training, volunteer time, funds, other resources) allocated to schools in the district?

12. At what levels does your district allocate private resources (school, classroom, teacher, and/or student level)?

13. For what purposes are the private resources used?

14. To what extent are private resources given for short-term versus long-term uses?

15. Do private revenues tend to be more or less restricted in their use than public resources? What types of restrictions exist on the use of private resources (legal, targeted, other restrictions)?

16. What are the legal facilitators or hindrances to the collection and use of private support?

17. What are the downsides to collecting private resources? What kinds of equity issues, if any, are raised by the collection of private support? Are there circumstances under which you have, or would have to, refuse a contribution?

18. To what extent do private resources provide leverage for additional public and private support? To what extent do private resources crowd out public support?

19. How has the role of private support in this district changed over time, if at all? What is the impetus for the changes?

20. We're particularly interested in the political climate and whether that facilitates or impedes your efforts. Please comment.

II. Schools in District

21. What makes individual schools more or less successful in bringing in private resources?

22. How does private giving differ at the school level versus the district level (different givers, different focus on in-kind versus monetary giving, other differences)?

23. What is the relative quantity of private resources received directly by the district versus directly by the individual schools?

24. Which schools in your district are particularly successful in attracting private support (including monetary and in-kind support)? Is it okay for us to contact them?

C. Local Education Foundation Interview Protocol

This appendix presents the protocol we used to gain an LEF perspective on private giving to public schools. The protocol was used primarily as background information in preparing this report. This protocol also helped us to gain a better understanding of LEF objectives.

1. When was the foundation established? Who initiated the establishment of the foundation?

2. Did the foundation receive any outside advice or assistance when it was established (from national LEF headquarters, consultants, others)?

3. What was the impetus for establishing the foundation?

4. What are the goals and mission of the foundation?

5. Have the functions of the foundation changed over time? If so, in what ways?

6. Does the foundation have any full-time or part-time employees?

7. What methods or techniques does the foundation use to raise resources for the district?

8. What types of resources are received by the foundation and from what types of givers? (Interviewer probed for the following: business, parents, philanthropic foundations, others.) To what extent does the foundation receive in-kind versus monetary private support?

9. How does the foundation interact with individual schools and, specifically, other organizations that attract private support at the school level? To what extent do the various organizations complement or compete with each other?

10. How does the foundation interact with the school district and, specifically, with district efforts to raise private support?

11. Can you quantify the private resources the foundation has received?

12. How are decisions made about spending foundation funds? How are foundation funds allocated across schools in the district?

13. What kinds of projects are funded by the foundation?

14. What factors/features influence the success of your foundation? And would those factors/features apply to LEFs more generally? (Interviewer probed for the following: socioeconomic statistics of the community, business and political environment, other factors.)

15. Does the LEF belong to a national level organization? If so, what kind of support does the organization provide? What should it provide that it doesn't?

D. Study Results on Local Education Foundations

Local education foundations are garnering increasing attention in both the popular press and research literature. In this appendix, we review the literature, as well as our findings from phone interviews with LEF representatives associated with three districts in our sample and interviews with district and school personnel.

The research literature examines the growth of LEFs, where LEFs are likely to be formed, and the level of support they raise. The emerging view is that the number of LEFs is growing and LEFs are providing districts with more flexible funding, but they also may be leading to greater inequities between wealthy and poor districts (although it has been argued that LEFs can also actually help close the gaps between higher-income and lower-income districts). In comparison with the literature, our interviews focused more closely on how LEFs raise funds and the processes by which they allocate funds.

Literature Review

In this section, we provide information from our search of published reports, journal articles, and the popular press. The following summaries provide a quick overview of the recent growth of LEFs, the dollar value of money raised by LEFs, and the characteristics of the districts that form successful LEFs.

Growth in the Number of LEFs

The consensus is that the number of LEFs is growing throughout the country, particularly in California. Merz and Frankel (1995) conducted a multistate analysis of foundation activity based on a survey of school districts and interviews with individuals involved with foundations. The study found that the vast majority of foundations have been formed since 1989, with California having the longest history with them. Brunner and Sonstelie (1997) used IRS data and the required registration of nonprofits operating in California and found widespread use of educational foundations in the state; more than 500 such foundations were in operation in 1995 in 1,001 school districts. Addonizio (1999) studied the growth of LEFs in Michigan and found that the number increased from just five in 1981 to 153 by 1997.

Amounts Raised by LEFs

There is less of a consensus regarding the *effectiveness* of LEFs in raising funds. Merz and Frankel (1995) found that whereas amounts raised through individual foundations in 1992 to 1993 ranged from $200 to $1 million, 20 percent of foundations reported raising only $10,000 to $40,000, and only 7 percent raised $100,000 or more during that period.

Studies by McLaughlin (1988) and Brown and Rinehart (1991) suggest that most LEFs raise small amounts of money and therefore are more effective as public relations tools than revenue-raising tools. Brunner and Sonstelie's research in California showed that LEFs raise more revenue for schools than do other types of nonprofit organizations supporting K–12 education. LEFs in California raised $28.9 million in 1992, followed by PTAs at $27.7 million, and booster clubs at $19.3 million. A recent analysis published in the *Los Angeles Times* (Fox, 2001) profiled the amounts raised by several Los Angeles–area LEFs in 1998. The amounts ranged from a low of $13,960 raised by the Wilsona/Lake Los Angeles Foundation for Student Excellence to a high of $5,258,199 raised by the Los Angeles Educational Partnership.

Merz and Frankel, Brunner and Sonstelie, and Addonizio all conclude that foundation contributions represent a small percentage of revenue in all but a handful of schools, providing very small amounts of money compared with school district budgets, and therefore have little effect on the per-pupil amounts available in districts.[1] However, research by Crampton and Bauman (1998) led to a different conclusion. Based on case study methods using six schools across three Colorado districts with distinct demographic profiles, Crampton and Bauman's research suggests that entrepreneurship activities, such as developing a LEF, did in fact have a disequalizing impact on intradistrict and interdistrict fiscal equity.

Where LEFs Are Formed

Merz and Frankel found that LEFs have been formed successfully in a range of communities. And, although affluent communities are not much more likely to

---

[1]In California, some parents have argued in court, so far unsuccessfully, that the LEFs that are being set up in some districts are a means to circumvent court equity decisions.

have LEFs, their LEFs are likely to raise relatively more money.[2] Addonizio found that districts with educational foundations, on average, enjoy higher unrestricted public revenue per pupil, greater enrollments, higher household income, and higher student achievement than their non-foundation counterparts.

Brunner and Sonstelie's (1997) research in California suggests that the per-pupil revenue from giving increases as average family income within a district increases.[3] For example, among school districts in California with average annual family incomes between $0 and $29,999, only 5.7 percent had a nonprofit organization that raised more than $25,000 in gross revenues. Furthermore, in those eight districts, total voluntary support for public education amounted to only $9 per student annually. In contrast, among districts with average annual family incomes of $70,000 or more, 79 percent had nonprofit organizations that raised more than $25,000 annually, with revenues totaling more than $240 per student.

A recent report in the *Los Angeles Times* (Fox, 2001) argued that foundations in wealthier districts in the Los Angeles region raise much more money per capita than foundations in less-wealthy districts. For example, the San Marino Schools Foundation (in a very affluent area) raised the equivalent of $381.09 per pupil in 1998. At the other end of the spectrum was the Long Beach Education Foundation (in a much less-affluent area), which raised the equivalent of only $1.06 per student.

Case Studies

As noted earlier, our study took a different approach than previous research in the field. Our primary purpose was to understand who gives to LEFs and through what mechanisms, the type of giving, and the end result of the giving (these research areas mirror the primary questions we used to examine the districts and schools through our interview protocols, shown in Appendices A through C).

---

[2]The high number of working professionals in one community almost doubled the average amount raised by the local district in a year: $46,260 raised in 1994 compared with other districts that raised an average of $25,280 that year. The presence or absence of a high number of retired people or families with no children did not affect the average amount raised.

[3]Merz and Frankel found that the number of nonprofits did not differ much across different economic communities. This difference in results may be due to Brunner and Sonstelie counting only those foundations with revenues greater than $25,000, whereas Merz and Frankel include all foundations. There may be some foundations in lower-income communities that are not raising enough revenue to appear in Brunner and Sonstelie's analyses.

Who Are the Givers?

The LEFs resemble the districts and schools in that their primary donors are parents and businesses. The LEF representatives we interviewed also emphasized the importance of community members, specifically those individuals who serve on foundation boards. Those individuals may wear many hats by being actual donors (of money or in-kind services), by working as foundation staff (in planning events or contacting potential donors), or by serving in an advisory role (for example, determining how money should be spent).

How Do They Give?

The three methods of contacting potential givers, mentioned by all LEF staff members, were mail solicitation/membership drives, personal contacts, and special events. All three techniques were also noted by some, if not all, of the schools and districts. Mail solicitations are typically targeted toward parents and local businesses, particularly if they have given in the past. The LEF representatives were also community members and businesspeople, and utilized their connections in trying to build support for the foundation and district. LEFs helped in hosting a number of fund-raising events, ranging from wine auctions to celebrity performances.

What Do They Give?

All three respondents noted that the majority, if not all, of their gifts are monetary donations, which is quite different from the schools and districts that are more likely to receive in-kind contributions. In terms of in-kind donations, all three LEFs greatly valued the volunteer time given by those serving on advisory boards (and resource boards) of the LEFs. None of the three respondents mentioned any sort of in-kind material donations.

How Are the Resources Allocated?

All three LEFs reported having formal grant awarding processes and grant committees for overseeing the distribution of funds to the schools. Typically these grants were in the form of requests for proposals (RFPs) for which individual teachers could apply. These "mini-grants" were generally open, in that teachers could propose a range of ideas for funding and the LEFs would try to award grants to teachers across the district.

Two respondents mentioned that their goal is to serve as many students and schools as possible. One LEF focused on supporting the arts while another's top priority was providing school uniforms, and the allocation of funds by both of these LEFs was more flexible once those primary needs had been met. LEFs also reported having a dialogue with the district and/or individual schools regarding their funding priorities.

The LEFs have much more contact with district staff than they do with individual schools, and all of the LEF interviewees reported having good relations with the districts they serve. Relations with individual schools were not as consistent—only one LEF representative mentioned having good relations with schools and regularly meeting with school principals and PTA presidents in the district. One of the other respondents noted having little contact with schools, although she hoped to have more contact with them in the future.

One issue that arose in our interviews with representatives from the schools, districts, and LEFs was the competition among each entity that resulted from multiple individuals approaching the same potential donors at the same time.

Conclusions

Our findings are not consistent with what the popular press has been reporting about LEFs. Although it may be true that they are growing in number, of the three foundations (out of four) we studied, only one is currently playing a significant role in raising funds and resources for its respective school district, one is on the verge of becoming an extremely important player, and one has only a limited role.[4]

Nevertheless, the concept of LEFs is very appealing to other districts—one of the remaining two districts in our sample that does not have a foundation is in the process of developing one, and the other district said it would like to start one but is worried that the selection process for board members might become too political.[5]

---

[4]The LEF that did not participate in our study also has only a limited role, according to the district with which it is associated.

[5]A couple of recent research studies have examined how to create and sustain education foundations. A study by Useem (1999) examines the governance and operation of LEFs, the relationship between LEFs and districts, LEF strategies, core areas of their work, and conditions for promoting their effectiveness. A study by Muro (1995) focuses on suggestions for fund-raising. (See also California Consortium of Educational Foundations, 1994.)

LEFs may be a good metaphor for private giving in general—the amounts they raise may not be large, but every additional dollar that comes into the schools through the LEFs is highly valued.

E. Source Citations for the Private-Giving Matrix

This appendix presents source citations for each item in our private-giving matrix (see Chapter 4). This is not a comprehensive list of citations because some items in the matrix had multiple sources. For example, parents were noted as private givers in numerous instances. For those items, we selected a few representative citations to present here.

The numbers after each item in Table E.1 refer to the corresponding citations in the numbered list that follows.

Items noted with "SV" resulted from our site visits and not the literature review.

Table E.1

Source Citations for Private-Giving Matrix

Private Givers	Entity Channeling Private Resources	Mechanism to Attract Private Resources	Type of Private Giving	Use of Private Monetary Giving
Students 11	Local education foundation 12, 14, 25	Product sales 26	**IN-KIND**	**Current Operations**
Parents 8, 10, 21	Booster club 16	Special events 3	**Volunteer Time**	Professional development 12, 13
Local businesses 1, 4, 18	PTA 8, 12, 26	Grant applications 2, 16	Student instruction 16	Classroom teachers 15
Corporations 3, 9	PTO 20	Mail solicitation 16, 20	Student tutoring 10	Teacher aides 16, 20
Philanthropic foundations 20, 27	School-site/leadership council SV	Phone solicitation 16, 20	Student mentoring 23	Salary enhancement or stipends for existing teachers 12
Community-based organizations 20	Other school-based club/association 16	Personal contacts/ relationship building 24	Classroom support 8, 21	Other staff salaries 2, 12
Community members 2, 5, 14	Principal 6	Professional fund-raiser 12, 17	Student support services 23	Instructional materials 12
Professionals associations (SV)	District staff (SV)	Leasing of school facilities SV	Enrichment programs 5	School supplies/ equipment 12, 20
Colleges/ universities 3	Superintendent 20	Participation in scrip or Web site programs 4, 16	Family services SV	Curricular enrichment programs 5, 26
	Advisory board (SV)	School-business partnerships 20, 22	Staff training 23	Athletics 9
		K-12 – Higher education partnerships (SV)	School facilities 19, 27	Student transportation 16
			Administrative 16	School maintenance 12, 16
			School promotion (SV)	Student supplies 8
			After-school programs 23	Promotion of school/business partnerships 20
			Material Donations	Parent education programs (SV)
			Instructional materials 16	Health clinics (SV)
			Technology 3, 20	

Table E.1—Continued

Private Givers	Entity Channeling Private Resources	Mechanism to Attract Private Resources	Type of Private Giving	Use of Private Monetary Giving
Alumni 7		Local and national presentations (SV)	**Material Donations (cont.)**	**Current Operations (cont.)**
City government (SV)		Local newspaper advertising (SV)	School supplies/equipment 16	Early childhood education (SV)
Advocacy group (SV)		High-profile speakers/hosts (SV)	Student/family supplies (SV)	Special events (SV)
Federal agency (SV)		Link with city planning (SV)	Off-site facilities for events (SV)	
		Peer pressure (SV)	Food (SV)	**Technology**
			Awards/gift certificates 23	Computers/software 3, 4, 25
			MONETARY	**Capital Improvements**
			Donation 2	Building additions 1, 20
			Membership dues (SV)	Building enhancement 20
			Percentage of sales 4, 26	School beautification 4, 16
			Wills/bequests SV	Heating/air conditioning (SV)
			Scholarships 23	Sports facilities 16
			Paid endorsements/advertising revenue 9	Playground equipment 4
			User fees (SV)	Electrical wiring 3
			Leasing of facilities and services (SV)	Furniture (SV)

Note: SV = Categories derived from site visits.

1. Anderson, N., "Going Beyond the Bake Sale: More Parents Are Starting Up Private Foundations to Raise Funds for Teachers, Programs, and Repairs at Their Schools," *Los Angeles Times*, December 2, 1997, p. A1.

2. Becker, T., "Students, Parents Help Schools Raise Funds for Libraries," *Los Angeles Times*, May 11, 1998, p. B3.

3. Colvin, R. L., "Volunteers Wire 2,400 Schools on NetDay; Education: Thousands Help Lay Groundwork to Hook Up to the Internet," *Los Angeles Times*, March 10, 1996, p. A1.

4. Ellingwood, K., and P. Y. Hong,, "More Fund-Raisers Scrambling for Scrip Charities: Demise of a Distributor Highlights Dependency of Schools, Churches on the Certificates," *Los Angeles Times*, January 17, 1998, p. A1.

5. Fernandes, L., "Parents' Frustration Is Making Music," *The San Francisco Chronicle*, December 24, 1993, p. A20.

6. Gaines, P., "Putting Muscle into Good Intentions; Hands-on Help of 3,000 Workathon Volunteers Gives D.C. Schools a Face Lift," *The Washington Post*, April 19, 1998, p. B03.

7. Glass, J., "Donations Sought for Maury High's Computers," *The Virginian-Pilot and The Ledger-Star*, March 9, 1995, p. 14.

8. Graham, E., "Education: Parents Clean, Shovel, Even Teach, to Aid Schools," *The Wall Street Journal*, June 12, 1995, p. B1.

9. Groves, M., "Serving Kids... Up to Marketers; Should Schools Use Vending Machines and Corporate Contracts to Get Needed Cash?" *Los Angeles Times*, July 14, 1999, p. B2.

10. Hobbs, D., and T. Nguyen, "Schools Find More Dads Helping Out as Volunteers: Class Projects, Field Trips, Fund-Raising, and Not Least of All, Their Children Benefit When Fathers Give," *Los Angeles Times*, February 9, 1998, p. B2.

11. Kowsky, K., "Many Schools Now Count on Private Donors for Extra Funds; Education: The Contributions from Foundations Supplement Budgets in a Time of Declining State Appropriations., but Critics Say the Efforts Also Widen the Gap Between Rich and Poor Districts," *Los Angeles Times*, June 12, 1992, p. B3.

12. Loar, R., and J. Bean, "Irvine Education Foundation's Role May Grow," *Los Angeles Times*, January 6, 1995, p. B2.

13. Loar, R., and J. Bean, "Orange County in Bankruptcy: Funds Raised for Schools to Buy Extras May Be Used for Basics," *Los Angeles Times,* December 16, 1994, p. A27.

14. Mathews, J., "More Public Schools Using Private Dollars; In Affluent U.S. Communities, Foundations Provide Funding," *The Washington Post,* August 28, 1994, p. A01.

15. Merz C., and S. S. Frankel, *Private Funds for Public Schools: A Study of School Foundations,* Tacoma, Washington: University of Puget Sound, 1995.

16. Minton, T., et al., "Parents Pitching in to Save Our Schools: As Funds Get Slashed, Volunteers Provide Essentials Such as Lunches, Books, Uniforms," *The San Francisco Chronicle,* September 24, 1992, p. D3.

17. Moran, C., "School Foundations: Bucks Continue Here," *The San Diego Tribune,* April 1, 1999, p. A1.

18. Pool, B., "NetDay2 Gives Students Access to the World Education: Volunteers to Help 200 Schools to Go Online, The Confusion That Marked the First Effort Is Reduced," *Los Angeles Times,* October 13, 1996, p. B4.

19. Renwick, L., and H. Weinstein, "Helpers Spruce Up Valley Schools; Volunteerism: Effort Involves Thousands of All Ages, Including the Entire Staff of a Business and Parents Who Joined Their Parents to Scrub, Paint and Plant," *Los Angeles Times,* May 19, 1996, p. A1.

20. Richardson, L., "Bridging the Gap: With School Districts Increasingly Strapped for Money, Individuals and Companies Are Giving Time and Materials," *Los Angeles Times,* December 22, 1994, pp. J8.

21. Schevitz, T., "Schools Pressuring Parents: Public, Private Campuses Want More Volunteers, Donations," *The San Francisco Chronicle,* September 23, 1997, p. A1.

22. Thomas-Lester, A., "Getting Help for the Business of Schools, *The Washington Post,* February 16, 2000, p. M19.

23. Timpane, M. P., and L. M. McNeil, *Business Impact on Education and Child Development Reform: A Study Prepared by the Committee for Economic Development,* New York: Committee for Economic Development, 1991.

24. Van Duch, M., "Schools Look Beyond PTAs to Raise Money," *Chicago Tribune,* May 15, 1995.

98

25. Vander Weele, M., "Schools Build Fund-Raising Foundations," *Chicago Sun-Times,* January 19, 1992.

26. Walker, T., "Sell, You Parents, Sell! Families: Don't Look Now, but Parents Have Become the Fund-raising Foot Soldiers for Schools and Youth Activities," *The Orange County Register,* October 14, 1999, p. E01.

27. Warchol, R., "Volunteers to Help Spruce up Schools," *Los Angeles Times,* September 16, 1997, p. B3.

Bibliography

Addonizio, M. F., "New Revenues for Public Schools: Alternatives to Broad-Based Taxes," in W. J. Fowler, ed., *Selected Papers in School Finance, 1997–99*, Washington, D.C.: U.S. Department of Education, Office of Educational Research and Improvement, NCES 1999-334, 1999, pp. 89–110.

Anderson, N., "Going Beyond the Bake Sale: More Parents Are Starting Up Private Foundations to Raise Funds for Teachers, Programs and Repairs at Their Schools," *Los Angeles Times*, December 2, 1997, p. A1.

Andreoni, J., "Giving with Impure Altruism: Applications to Charity and Recardian Equivalence," *Journal of Political Economy*, Vol. 82, 1989, pp. 1447–1458.

Beadie, N., "The Limits of Standardization and the Importance of Constituencies: Historical Tensions in the Relationship Between State Authority and Local Control," in N. D. Theobald and B. Malen, eds., *Balancing Local Control and State Responsibility for K–12 Education*, Larchmont, N.Y.: Eye on Education, 2000.

Becker, G., "A Theory of Social Interactions," *Journal of Political Economy*, Vol. 82, 1974, pp. 1063–1094.

Becker, T., "Students, Parents Help Schools Raise Funds for Libraries," *Los Angeles Times*, May 11, 1998, p. B3.

Benning, V., "Parents; Crucial Volunteers; Help Is Key to Smooth-Running Schools," *The Washington Post*, August 26, 1999, p. J1.

Boland Johnson, N., "Schools Need Volunteers to Help Youngsters Improve Reading Skills," *The Boston Globe*, August 29, 1999.

Bradley, A., "Local Fund-Raising Prompts Larger Questions About Equity," *Education Week*, October 11, 1995.

Brown, J., and Rinehart, J., "Private Foundations: An Empowerment Tool," *Record*, Spring/Summer 1991, pp. 53–57.

Brunner, E., and J. Sonstelie, "Coping with Serrano: Voluntary Contributions to California's Local Public Schools," paper presented at 89th Annual Conference on Taxation, National Tax Association, October 1997.

_____, "School Finance Reform and Voluntary Fiscal Federalism," unpublished working paper, San Diego State University (Brunner) and University of California, Santa Barbara (Sonstelie), 1999.

California Consortium of Educational Foundations, *Starting an Educational Foundation*, 1994, available at www.cceflink.org.

Cary, J., "Volunteers Give Bilingual Students Individual Attention," *Chicago Tribune*, March 15, 1998.

Chmelynski, C., "Non-profit Foundations Raise Millions for Schools," National School Board Association, February 23, 1999. Available at www.nsba.org/sbn/1999/022399-all.htm (last accessed August 10, 2001).

Colvin, R. L., "Volunteers Wire 2,500 Schools on NetDay; Education: Thousands Help Lay Groundwork to Hook Up to the Internet," *Los Angeles Times*, March 10, 1996, p. A1.

Crampton, F. E., and P. Bauman, "A New Challenge to Fiscal Equity: Educational Entrepreneurship and Its Implications for States, Districts, and Schools," paper presented at the American Educational Research Association, San Diego, Calif., 1998.

Dauber, S. L., and J. L. Epstein, "Parents' Attitudes and Practices of Involvement in Inner-City Elementary and Middle Schools," in N. Chavkin, ed., *Families and Schools in a Pluralistic Society*, Albany, N.Y.: State University of New York Press, 1993.

Dayton, J., ed., *The Allocation of Resources to Special Education and Regular Instruction in New York State*, Thousand Oaks, Calif.: Corwin Press, Inc., 1999.

_____, "Recent Litigation and Its Impact on the State-Local Power Balance: Liberty and Equity in Governance, Litigation, and the School Finance Policy Debate," in N. D. Theobald and B. Malen, eds., *Balancing Local Control and State Responsibility for K–12 Education*, Larchmont, N.Y.: Eye on Education, 2000.

de Luna, P., "Local Education Foundations: Right for Many Schools," *Phi Delta Kappan*, Vol. 79, No. 5, 1998, pp. 385–389.

Dornbusch, S. M., and P. L. Ritter, "Parents of High School Students: A Neglected Resource," *Educational Horizons*, No. 66, 1988, pp. 75–77.

Duncan, B., "Modeling Charitable Contributions of Time and Money," *Journal of Public Economics*, No. 72, 1999, pp. 213–242.

Eccles, J. S., "Family Involvement in Children's and Adolescents' Schooling," in A. Booth and J. Dunn, eds., *Family-School Links: How Do They Affect Educational Outcomes?* Mahwah, N.J.: Lawrence Erlbaum, 1996.

Ellingwood, K., and P. Y. Hong, "More Fund-Raisers Scrambling for Scrip Charities: Demise of a Distributor Highlights Dependency of Schools, Churches on the Certificates," *Los Angeles Times*, January 17, 1998, p. A1.

Epstein, J. L., "School/Family/Community Partnerships: Caring for the Children We Share," *Phi Delta Kappan*, Vol. 76, No. 9, 1995, pp. 701–712.

Epstein, J. L., and S. Lee, "National Patterns of School and Family Connections in the Middle Grades," in B. A. Ryan and G. R. Adams, eds., *The Family-School Connection: Theory, Research, and Practice*, Newbury Park, Calif.: Sage, 1995.

Ferguson, V. A., "Foundation Set Up to Foster Teaching: Local Group Will Give Out $500 Grants to Encourage Innovation in Education," *The Hartford Courant*, January 17, 1995, p. B4.

Fernandes, L., "Parents' Frustration Is Making Music," *The San Francisco Chronicle*, December 25, 1993, p. A20.

Fernandez, R., and R. Rogerson, *Education Finance Reform and Investment in Human Capital: Lessons from California*, Cambridge, Mass.: National Bureau of Economic Research, Working Paper No. W5369, 1995.

Fischel, W. A., "Did Serrano Cause Proposition 13?" *National Tax Journal*, Vol. 42, 1989, pp. 465–473.

_____, "Property Taxation and Tiebout Model: Evidence for the Benefit View from Zoning and Voting," *Journal of Economic Literature*, No. 30, 1992, pp. 171–177.

_____, *Proposition 13 and Local Self Government*, Dartmouth College, Hanover, N.H., 1993.

Fox, S., "Private Fund-Raising for Schools Runs Gamut," *Los Angeles Times*, April 15, 2001, p. B1.

Gaines, P., "At Schools Cleanup, Parents Absent: Few Show Up to Help with the Finishing Touches Before the First Day of Classes," *The Washington Post*, September 21, 1997, p. B9.

_____, "Putting Muscle into Good Intentions; Hands-on Help of 3,000 Workathon Volunteers Gives D.C. Schools a Face Lift," *The Washington Post*, April 19, 1998, p. B3.

GAO, *see* U.S. General Accounting Office.

Glass, J. "Donations Sought for Maury High's Computers," *The Virginian-Pilot and The Ledger-Star*, March 9, 1995, p. 14.

Glazer, A., and K. A. Konrad, "A Signaling Explanation for Charity," *American Economic Review*, No. 86, 1996, pp. 1019–1028.

Gray, M., and L. Ondaatje, R. Fricker, S. Geschwind, C. Goldman, T. Kaganoff, A. Robyn, M. Sundt, L. Vogelgesang, and S. Klein, *Combining Service and Learning in Higher Education*, Santa Monica, Calif.: RAND, MR-998-EDU, 1999.

Graham, E., "Education: Parents Clean, Shovel, Even Teach, to Aid Schools," *The Wall Street Journal*, June 12, 1995, p. B1.

Groves, M., "Serving Kids Up to Marketers; Should Schools Use Vending Machines and Corporate Contracts to Get Needed Cash?" *Los Angeles Times*, July 14, 1999, p. B2.

Harbaugh, W. T., "What Do Donations Buy? A Model of Philanthropy Based on Prestige and Warm Glow," *Journal of Public Economics*, No. 67, 1998, pp. 269–284.

Helft, M., "200 Volunteers Connect with Their Schools; Computers: As Part of NetDay 96, High-Tech Specialists, Area Businesses and Parents Donate Time, Materials to Give Students Access to the Internet," *Los Angeles Times,* March 10, 1996, p. B5.

Helman, S. W., "Helping Hand for Schools: Town Foundations Provide Vital Funding," *The Boston Globe,* February 13, 2000.

Hickrod, A. G., E. R. Hines, G. P. Anthony, J. A. Dively, and G. B. Pruyne, "The Effect of Constitutional Litigation on Educational Finance: A Preliminary Analysis," *Journal of Education Finance*, No. 18, 1992, pp. 180–210.

Hobbs, D., and T. Nguyen, "Schools Find More Dads Helping Out Volunteers: Class Projects, Field Trips, Fund-Raising, and Not Least of All, Their Children Benefit When Fathers Give," *Los Angeles Times,* February 9, 1998, p. B2.

Iudica, D. E., "Schools Find New Funds; Non-profit Foundations Are Growing in Popularity," *The Boston Globe,* October 13, 1991.

Johnson, T., "Fewer Moms Able to Help Out in Schools Education: Volunteers Once Filled the Jobs Left Vacant by Budget Cuts on the Palos Verdes Peninsula, but Now Many Are Returning to Work," *Los Angeles Times,* June 17, 1996, p. B10.

Kaufman, M., "Coca-Cola Tries to Cap Exclusive School Deals," *Washington Post,* 2001, p. A2.

Kowsky, K., "Many Schools Now Count on Private Donors for Extra Funds," *Los Angeles Times,* June 12, 1992, p. B3.

Kummerer, W., "$5,000 Grant Helps Parents Read to Kids," *Chicago Tribune,* January 19, 2000.

Lareau, A., *Home Advantage: Social Class and Parental Intervention in Elementary Education*, Philadelphia: Falmer Press, 1989.

Legislative Analyst's Office, *Analysis of the Budget Bill: An Historical Perspective of Education Funding*, Sacramento, Calif., 2000.

Loar, R., and J. Bean, "Orange County in Bankruptcy: Funds Raised for Schools to Buy Extras May Be Used for Basics," *Los Angeles Times,* December 16, 1994, p. A27.

_____, "Irvine Education Foundation's Role May Grow," *Los Angeles Times,* January 6, 1995, p. B2.

Lucadamo, J., "Glenview Schools Try to Build Foundation," *Chicago Tribune,* December 11, 1989.

Mamokhin, G., *Corporate Investment in Education: Motivational Factors and Trends in Direct Giving,* unpublished dissertation, University of Southern California, Los Angeles, 2000.

Manwaring, R. L., and S. M. Sheffin, *The Effects of Educational Equalization Litigation on the Levels of Funding: An Empirical Analysis*, Department of Economics, University of California, Davis, 1994.

_____, *Litigation, School Finance Reform, and Aggregate Educational Spending*, Department of Economics, University of California, Davis, 1995.

Mathews, J., "More Public Schools Using Private Dollars; In Affluent U.S. Communities, Foundations Provide Funding," *The Washington Post*, August 28, 1995, p. A1.

McGuire, C., "Business Involvement in Education in the 1990s," in *Education and Politics for the New Century*, D. Mitchell and M. Goertz, eds., New York: Palmer Press, 1990.

McLaughlin, M., "Business and Public Schools: New Patterns of Support," in D. Monk and J. Underwood, eds., *Micro Level School Finance: Issues and Implications for Policy*, Cambridge, Mass.: Ballinger, 1988, pp. 63–80.

McNatt, L., "Private Money Sought to Help Public Schools," *The Virginian-Pilot and The Ledger-Star*, April 26, 1995.

Meade, E. J., "Foundations and the Public Schools: An Impressionistic Retrospective 1960–1990," *Phi Delta Kappan*, Special Report, October 1991.

Merz, C., and S. S. Frankel, *Private Funds for Public Schools: A Study of School Foundations*, Tacoma, Washington: University of Puget Sound, 1995.

_____, "School Foundations: Local Control or Equity Circumvented?" *School Administrator*, No. 54, 1997, pp. 28–31.

Minton, T., R. D. Givhan, S. Whiting, S. Rubin, and J. Carroll, "Parents Pitching in to Save Our Schools: As Funds Get Slashed, Volunteers Provide Essentials Such as Lunches, Books, Uniforms," *The San Francisco Chronicle*, September 25, 1992, p. D3.

Moran, C., "School Foundations: Bucks Continue Here," *The San Diego Tribune*, April 10, 1999, p. A1.

Mount, C., "Angry Taxpayers Aiding Schools on Own Terms with Foundations," *Chicago Tribune*, November 17, 1993.

Mullins, D., and Joyce, P., "Tax Expenditure Limitations and State and Local Fiscal Structure: An Empirical Assessment," *Public Budgeting and Finance*, Spring 1996, pp. 75–101.

Muro, J., *Creating and Funding Educational Foundations: A Guide for Local School Districts*, Boston: Allyn and Bacon, 1995.

Nakamura, D., "Educational Priorities Take a New Turn; Parents Raised Funds to Build Running Tracks at Two Elementary Schools," *The Washington Post*, September 14, 1997, p. V3.

National Center for Education Statistics, *Digest of Education Statistics 1998,* Washington, D.C.: U.S. Department of Education, May 1999.

Pindyck, R., and D. Rubinfeld, *Microeconomics,* New York: Macmillan Publishing Company, 1992.

Pool, B., "NetDay2 Gives Students Access to the World Education: Volunteers to Help 200 Schools to Go Online; The Confusion That Marked the First Effort Is Reduced," *Los Angeles Times,* October 13, 1996, p. B5.

Pugh, T., *Rural School Consolidation in New York State, 1795–1993: A Struggle for Control,* unpublished dissertation, Syracuse University, Syracuse, N.Y., 1994.

Renwick, L., and H. Weinstein, "Helpers Spruce Up Valley Schools," *Los Angeles Times,* May 19, 1996, p. A1.

Richardson, L., "Bridging the Gap: With School Districts Increasingly Strapped for Money, Individuals and Companies Are Giving Time and Materials," *Los Angeles Times,* December 22, 1994, p. J8.

Saslow, L., "Foundations Give 'Extras' to Schools," *The New York Times,* October 16, 1994, p. L1.

Schevitz, T., "Schools Pressuring Parents: Public, Private Campuses Want More Volunteers, Donations," *The San Francisco Chronicle,* September 23, 1997, p. A1.

Silva, F., and J. Sonstelie, "Did Serrano Cause a Decline in School Spending?" *National Tax Journal,* No. 48, 1993, pp. 199–215.

Theobald, N. D., and L. O. Picus, "Living with Equal Amounts of Less: Experiences of States with Primarily State-Funded School Systems," *Journal of Education Finance,* Vol. 17, No. 1, 1991, pp. 1–6.

Thomas-Lester, A., "Getting Help for the Business of the Schools," *The Washington Post,* February 16, 2000, p. M19.

Tijerina, E. S., "Fund Gives Education Needed Lift," *Chicago Tribune,* January 6, 1992.

Timpane, M. P., and L. M. McNeill, *Business Impact on Education and Child Development Reform: A Study Prepared by the Committee for Economic Development,* New York: Committee for Economic Development, 1991.

Useem, E., *From the Margins to the Center of School Reform: A Look at the Work of Local Education Funds in Seventeen Communities,* Washington, D.C.: Public Education Network, 1999.

U.S. General Accounting Office, *Public Education: Commercial Activities in Schools,* Washington, D.C., HEHS-00-1561, September 8, 2000.

_____, *School Facilities: The Condition of American Schools,* Washington, D.C., HEHSS-95-61, 1995.

Van Duch, M., "Schools Look Beyond PTAs to Raise Money," *Chicago Tribune,* May 15, 1995.

Vander Weele, M., "Schools Build Fund-raising Foundations," *Chicago Sun-Times*, January 19, 1992.

Walker, T., "Sell, You Parents, Sell! Families: Don't Look Now, but Parents Have Become the Fund-raising Foot Soldiers for Schools and Youth Activities," *The Orange County Register*, October 15, 1999, p. E1.

Warchol, R., "Volunteers to Help Spruce Up Schools," *Los Angeles Times*, September 16, 1997, p. B3.

Weinstein, H., and L. Renwick, "Help? A Ton; 4,000 Volunteers Roll Up Their Sleeves to Spruce Up Schools, Community Centers," *Los Angeles Times*, May 19, 1996, p. A1.

White, K. A., "Local Funds Playing Larger Roles in Reform," *Education Week*, February 11, 2000.

Willman, M. L., "Decade of La Canada Fund-Raising: Education Foundation Celebrates a Milestone," *Los Angeles Times*, June 1, 1989.

Yin, R. K., *Case Study Research Design and Methods*, Applied Social Research Methods Series, Vol. 5, Newbury Park, Calif.: Sage Publications, 1994.